The COLORADO Angling Guide

by

Chuck Fothergill and
Bob Sterling

Stream Stalker Publishing
Aspen, Colorado

First Edition
2 3 4 5 6 7 8 9

Published by:
Stream Stalker Publishing
Box 1010
Aspen, Colorado 81612

ISBN: 0-9614704-0-2

Set in Chelmsford type by Dianne Borneman of Shadow Canyon Graphics, Evergreen, Colorado, and printed by Walsworth Publishing Company, Marceline, Missouri, U.S.A.

Library of Congress Catalog Card
Number 85-61624

Contents

INTRODUCTION

We hope that you find this angling guide informative and helpful. It concentrates on those rivers of Colorado designated by the Colorado Division of Wildlife as either "Gold Medal" or "Wild Trout" waters. Gold Medal is defined as ". . . the highest quality aquatic habitat for trout that exists in Colorado which offers the greatest potential for trophy trout fishing and angling success." Wild Trout water is defined as "Waters which support a naturally reproducing and self-sustaining trout population without artificial stocking. Artificial stocking of such waters will occur only under emergency conditions."

All of the Gold Medal waters have been designated with special regulations that are published and available from license agents and Division of Wildlife representatives throughout the state. The reader should be aware, however, that not all Wild Trout and Gold Medal water have public access. There are several rivers so designated on which fishing is not permitted, so you must be careful not to make assumptions of access because of special designations or regulations.

Colorado contains more than 7,000 miles of trout streams. There are 2,850 cold water lakes and 360 warm water reservoirs. This book includes only a fraction of them—those that are usually considered as destination waters for the serious fisherman and for anglers who wish the opportunity to catch sizable trout in reasonably good numbers. For all of the waters not presented here, local information can be obtained from tackle stores, Division of Wildlife offices, and representatives of the U.S. Forest Service.

There are undoubtedly streams you have heard about that you will not find in this guide—names like Elk, Pine, Yampa, Mancos, Piedra, Animas, and San Juan. These certainly are rivers of interest to the angler, but in our opinion, they do not have the attributes needed to be included with the rivers given special designation by the Division of Wildlife.

We have tried to gather and present our information about Colorado fishing as accurately as possible. We plan to publish future editions of the guide as changes to it become necessary. The fish and insects of each watershed will probably remain somewhat constant in character through the years, as nature tends to be patient and thoughtful in its evolutionary process. Man, on the other hand, often finds delay and contemplation to be regressive inaction, and not to be tolerated in a progressive society. We therefore do not know for sure that today's county road won't be tomorrow's interstate freeway, nor can we forecast that today's free-flowing river won't be tomorrow's stillwater reservoir. In any event, we trust that changes won't be so rapid as to cause serious disappointments in your searchings for that special place and that special trout.

A few topics fall into the category of general interest, and we present them here rather than repeating the same subject matter in each chapter.

Fishing Regulations

The state agency controlling the administration of Colorado's fish and fishing regulations has gone to a great deal of effort to provide the fishing public with detailed rules concerning the sport we enjoy. We are fortunate in Colorado to have a wildlife agency that is truly concerned about the survival of wild trout, the preservation of endangered species, the protection of fish habitat, and the relationship between the private land owner and the sportsman.

The fishing regulations can change each year, and it is the responsibility of the Colorado Division of Wildlife to publish those regulations. We have, therefore, avoided including them in this guide. We do, however, strongly suggest that before you fish any body of water in Colorado, refer to the regulations to determine what rules apply.

Many waters are regulated to improve the fishery, and therefore carry special regulations. To avoid the embarrassment and cost of being summoned for violation of the rules, check ahead of time. The regulation books are available at no cost from license agents and from wildlife offices.

Tackle Shops

In many areas of the state, it is possible to hire a fishing guide to help you learn the local waters and fishing techniques. Guides spend a great deal of time on their local waters and know the latest information about local conditions. Even if hired for only one day to help you "get your feet wet" in a new river, they are usually a worthwhile investment.

Some guide services provide float trip fishing from either hard-keel or inflatable boats. This can prove to be an interesting and productive way to cover more water than you could hope to do by wading, and many times puts you over fish not reached by the wading angler.

Several tackle shops throughout Colorado are set up to rent equipment should you leave home without it entirely, or if you brought your rod but forgot your reel. Who of us hasn't experienced that embarrassing dilemma? So don't hesitate to ask if rental gear is available.

Private Property

Wouldn't it be wonderful if all trout streams flowed entirely through public property? We would never be concerned with fences, we would never have to question the propriety of our presence on any body of water, and there would be fewer anglers per acre of water because we would be more widely distributed up and down the river.

Well, life isn't perfect, and private property does exist and must be respected. In some states, the bottom of a trout stream is public domain, and once you set foot there, you can proceed up and downstream at will as long as you do not walk beyond the high-water mark. This is not the case in Colorado, however. The streambed in a river is private property when the adjacent land is privately owned. Depending upon this riparian ownership, the streambed may be private halfway or fully across the stream. It is important, therefore, to always establish your right to fish a given piece of water before entering it.

A general ground rule to follow when an area is fenced is to consider it as private property. If it is not fenced, there is usually no reason why you cannot fish there. If it appears private, ask permission from the owner. Sometimes you will be denied permission, but at least make the effort— you might be surprised and gain access to some seldomly fished water. In most areas of Colorado, land owners respond favorably to polite requests for access to the river.

Signs on fences will tell you the owner's feeling toward privacy—"No Hunting, Fishing, or Trespassing" tells the story very well. Less restrictive signs will read, "Fishing by Permission Only." This verbiage is evidence that you are probably welcome to fish, but the property owner requires the opportunity to meet you and personally tell you his rules, restrictions, etc.

A situation where you are definitely welcome to fish is when a sign says "Fishing Permitted." Sometimes you will even find a stile built over the fence to facilitate your progress without tearing your waders. In some areas of the state, the Division of Wildlife has negotiated access leases with land owners. These accesses do allow you to get into the river and move about as necessary to fish, but they normally do not allow you to wander about at will through the hay meadows and cattle pastures!

When access is permitted, no matter what the reason, we should use extreme care to respect the property and its owner. The reason why we see too many "No Trespassing" signs posted is because people before us abused the privilege and the property. A rancher's land is his livelihood, and he must manage his business for his benefit first, and ours second.

Common sense rules to adhere to are as follows when on someone else's property:

1. Don't light fires.
2. Leave gates as you find them.
3. Avoid contact with livestock and pets.
4. Don't drop trash—carry it out.
5. Leave your pets in your car or at home.
6. Follow all verbal or written rules of the property.
7. Don't discharge firearms.
8. Don't damage trees, bushes, crops, or groundcover.
9. Don't block gates or drives with your vehicle.
10. Don't use the property for activities other than those agreed upon with the land owner.

Wading

As winter's snowpack melts under the progressively warming rays of spring and summer sunshine, the rivers of Colorado fill with water that swiftly rushes to the Atlantic and Pacific oceans. Although some melting occurs during the waning days of winter, the serious "runoff" commences from late April to mid-May, and continues to early July and as late as mid-August. High water during an average year peaks in mid-June and tapers off to normal flows sometime in July on most streams. Snowpacks in the

Rockies vary as much as tenfold from year to year, and runoff conditions vary accordingly. Because of the state's elevation, Colorado is the birthplace of more major rivers than any other state in the lower forty-eight. They include the Colorado, Arkansas, Platte, and Rio Grande.

Almost all streams in Colorado present an element of concern about safety to the angler wading them. Some areas in all streams are easy to wade, but as a general rule, fishermen would be wise to use wading equipment that will ensure a high degree of confidence and safety under all conditions. For fishing the rivers covered in this guide, we advise wearing chest waders with felt soles. There are, of course, exceptions, but it is better to be overprepared than poorly prepared.

Fooling fish during the runoff can be very difficult, particularly if you are using flies and lures. The turbidity, large volume, and high speed of the water make isolating your lure much more difficult for the trout than when flows are at normal levels. The situation is not necessarily a piece of cake for you either when you are trying to keep your feet stuck to the river bottom and the current wants to push them into the next county. Metal cleats of some form are strongly recommended under these conditions.

If you can plan your trip when the water is lower, your chances of catching fish are enhanced, and your chances of taking an involuntary bath are reduced. Under any circumstances, try to use good judgment when wading, and stay dry!

Float Fishing

If you plan to float any of Colorado's rivers without a professional guide or someone who knows the water, check with local tackle shops concerning the put-in and take-out points along the river, as they can change from year to year as river courses change or land use is altered. Check for difficulty, private property, and hazardous conditions for the time of year and stretch of river you plan to float. Take the time to scout the river thoroughly prior to putting in. Many times this can be done easily if there is a good road paralleling the river. Boulders, construction debris, downed trees, bridge abutments, rockslides, headgates, and barbed wire can be encountered suddenly but not avoided, and although such situations are rare, it takes only one such incident to ruin the trip!

Unless you know that you are on public property, do not beach your boat for less than emergency reasons. A private property owner may not appreciate your intrusion and may confront you for trespassing.

Another consideration when floating unfamiliar water is to allow yourself plenty of time to arrive at your take-out point before it turns dark. Personal experience with this problem prompts the suggestion! We pulled out of a river once at dusk without really being able to see where we were going, and not only did we have to offload our gear into a patch of muck at riverside, but we walked into an electrified barbed wire fence and were confronted by several cattle being held next to the river that evening. Had we planned better and been able to see better, we would have taken out at another corner of the bridge with no problem.

Flies and Lures

The fly patterns associated with each of the rivers are those which have proven themselves to be effective from year to year. These are the patterns most sold in local stores and most used by local anglers. Because we are concentrating on the waters of only one state, there will be some redundancy in patterns from river to river because of similarities of insect life. Some of the patterns are favorites throughout the Rocky Mountains, and others are familiar patterns used throughout the country. Lures fall into the same category with several designs being effective on most waters of the state.

We suggest that you inquire at local tackle shops for fly and lure suggestions that may be working especially well at the time you plan to fish nearby waters. Certain fly patterns can be very seasonal and localized to specific rivers at specific times, so it is a good idea to check with local anglers having current information.

A Little Help from Our Friends

The authors feel strongly about helping in the nationwide efforts to preserve trout fishing for this and future generations. Toward that goal, we have been active members of the national organization Trout Unlimited for many years. T.U. has been active since 1959 and has chapters in states throughout the country promoting and assisting with fishery and water protection, enhancement, and management. In cooperation with government agencies, Colorado T.U. members unselfishly give of their time and resources to do what they can to perpetuate good trout fishing in the state for residents and visitors alike.

We have listed here those communities in which Trout Unlimited chapters have been established. For further information on their activities and meeting schedules, you can contact local fishing tackle outlets who normally keep abreast of chapter events. Chapters in Colorado are:

Alamosa	Grand Junction
Arvada	Greeley
Aspen	Gunnison
Aurora	Littleton
Boulder	Longmont
Colorado Springs	Loveland
Denver	Montrose
Durango	Pagosa Springs
Estes Park	Steamboat Springs
Evergreen	Telluride
Frisco	Vail
Glenwood Springs	

Miscellaneous

All Colorado phone numbers listed in this guide will carry a prefix of 303. Those for other than Colorado will have the proper prefix listed.

Roads indicated will be hardtop and passable by passenger car unless noted to the contrary.

Part I:

Gold Medal, Wild Trout Rivers and Towns Along the Way

COLORADO OVERVIEW

Welcome to the fishing and associated pleasures of Colorado! We wish you the most pleasant of experiences while you are here, whether it be for only a few days or for the rest of your life. We hope that you will use the information in this guide to assist in planning your visits to the waters and communities we discuss, and we hope that you will find the information as factual as we believe it to be.

We have lived and fished in Colorado for many years. We have enjoyed the dry heat and bright sunshine of July while casting imitation Green Drakes to eagerly rising brown trout on the frigid water of the Frying Pan River. We have watched the rising sun splash yellow against the hillsides next to the Rio Grande after the aspen trees had changed color in cool, crisp October. We know the uncomfortable delight of hooking Gunnison River browns as the snow grows progressively deeper on our hat brims during a winter storm in early December.

We have been told a lot of fish stories over the years by a lot of fishermen in Colorado, and the tales are becoming more exciting all the time as more water is managed for the welfare of the fish rather than the appetite of the fisherman. The Colorado Division of Wildlife is doing an exemplary job of studying the needs of trout, and results of

11

these studies are prompting management policies that may bring back stories to rival those told in the "good old days."

For your fun, comfort, and safety, we want to present some general information that could enhance your Colorado experience. We do not wish to insult your intelligence or belittle your knowledge of the state, but first-time visitors may find an item or two of interest here!

History

The history of Colorado has been written about at great length on all levels, including the state, the counties, and even the smallest of towns. Colorado's background in contemporary history would start with the American Indian, who roamed and hunted freely over the state in the early 1800s. That is the time when exploration by the white man was taking place in southeast Colorado. Resident Indian tribes were distributed throughout the state as follows:

Northeast section—Shoshone
West, Southwest, and Central (the largest distribution)—
    Ute
Northeast—Cheyenne and Arapahoe
Southeast—Kiowa and Comanche

The Utes were known as the Blue Sky People, due to their living in the high mountains of Colorado. They were fine horsemen and were among the first North American Indians to acquire horses from the Spanish.

The first discovery of gold in the state took place at Central City in 1858. This started a gold and silver boom which lasted into the turn of the century. Silver was demonetized in 1893, and many mining camps were closed as a result.

From the late 1890s until the 1940s, the state relied on some mining, some tourism, but primarily ranching and agriculture as its economic base. With an affluent society starting to travel more easily and frequently after World War II, the ski industry began its rapid development to establish Colorado as a very popular destination in both winter and summer.

Many people make it a point to visit the state at least twice a year to take advantage of the wide spectrum of activities and special events that make Colorado so appealing.

Weather

As in many regions where mountains dominate the landscape, it is often said that if you don't like the weather now, wait ten minutes and it will change. Fortunately for Coloradans, this axiom isn't always true because they receive and enjoy a great deal of sunshine. Colorado is not known for dreary, overcast weather conditions!

It is not unusual or unexpected, however, to be playing tennis one minute and watching the rain build puddles in the forecourt a few minutes later. The interplay of mountain peaks and rain clouds can quickly cause a dry day to become wet, and warm air to become cold. These stormy conditions can be dangerous if you are caught outside with no shelter nearby, and without clothing to protect you from the cold and wet. Whenever you leave civilization to head for the high country, don't overlook the possibility of inclement weather, as afternoon showers commonly occur after the nicest morning sunshine you can imagine.

As a general rule during the summer months, you can expect daytime temperatures to be between 70 and 90 degrees F. in all mountainous areas discussed in this book, and you should expect nighttime temperatures to fall into the 40s. A sweater or heavy shirt is usually needed in early morning and late evening, and the time in between is strictly shirtsleeve weather.

With every 1,000 feet of rise in elevation, the temperature drops about 4 degrees F., which is the same as going approximately 350 miles north. Don't hesitate to throw another sweater into the suitcase!

Camping

A great number of tourists to this state enjoy camping as part of the outdoor activity they wish to experience on their visit to the mountains. The dry air, cool nights, and temperate days of summer and fall are ideally suited for sleeping under the stars, pitching a tent, or enjoying the comfort of a recreational vehicle.

Because much of today's camping is done in organized areas with some degree of developed facilities, it is important for our own comfort, and that of neighboring campers, to recognize what is available to us, and what we might do to enhance our experience. A few items for your information are listed here:

1. Use of fire may be restricted during high fire danger periods.

2. Campgrounds usually contain tables, toilets, trash removal, fire grates, and individual parking spurs.

3. Some campgrounds have drinking water, but if not, treat or boil water before use. Boil at least ten minutes.

4. Most campgrounds have a maximum use limit of fourteen days.

5. Use biodegradable soap for dishwashing or bathing, and dispose of water away from streams.

6. Use a rock fire circle to protect from wind blowing hot embers.

7. When leaving the campsite, be sure to drown fires thoroughly with water. Make sure the entire fire is soaked.

8. If you intend to use an organized campground, try to select a site by noon in areas with heavy use.

9. Firewood is not provided at campsites, and deadfall should be used. It is usually easily obtainable outside the campground itself.

10. A fee is usually charged at campgrounds that provide

drinking water. Fees are deposited in envelopes provided at the campground entrance.

Hiking

For hiking or backpacking in anything more than a casual manner, it's a good idea to obtain U.S. Geological Survey 7.5 minute topographic maps. The address is Denver Federal Center, Box 25286, Denver, 80225. An index to the topo maps is usually available at U.S. Forest Service offices in the district applicable to your chosen hiking route.

Don't forget the normal hiking precautions when going out for more than a casual stroll. Take along some snacks, a flashlight, matches, a jacket or sweater, rain gear, proper shoes or boots, first aid kit, proper maps, sunscreen, sunglasses, drinking water, and don't neglect telling someone where you plan to hike and when you expect to return.

During electrical storms, stay inside your vehicle if possible. If not, find a dense stand of timber, crouch between rocks in a boulder field, or, if possible, take shelter in a cave.

Always be prepared for bad weather, as mountain storms can start almost without warning and can cause serious problems.

If you get lost, try to remain calm and find a high point from which to get your bearings and plan a route to safety. If you find a trail, stay on it heading downhill. Same with a stream—follow it downstream. If you wish to make a signal noise or light flashes, remember that three of either will attract attention to your plight.

Critters

Almost all trout fishing in Colorado is enjoyed above

5,000 feet. Fortunately for the angler, poisonous snakes don't often inhabit terrain above 5,000 feet. This doesn't imply that they are never present at higher elevations, but odds are the fisherman is unlikely to encounter one. We've heard stories of their existence in the rocky canyons along rivers between 5,000 and 6,000 feet, but few contacts are reported from such areas. The point of these remarks is that you don't have to look over your shoulder for rattlers while trying to concentrate on your fishing. On the other hand, in the lower elevations, it's not unwise to be somewhat watchful and aware of their possible presence.

Occasionally a small water snake or garter snake will wiggle out of the path on your approach, but we consider such a sighting an interesting bonus to the day's total experience, not something to be fearfully anticipated or regretfully remembered!

One creature of the outdoors we do take a bit more seriously is the tick. This small (⅛ to 3/16 inch) parasite will gladly take advantage of your body as a place to bore in and spend some time, and the warmer the place, the more he likes it. A relative of spiders and scorpions rather than insects, the tick lives under leaves and in rotten wood, and usually finds his way to our tender epidermis as we walk through riverside alders and willows or sit on a log stump for a rest. Before modern antibiotics and cures were developed, the tick had given death-causing Rocky Mountain Spotted Fever to some of its unfortunate victims. Repellents used for chiggers will usually work against ticks.

Ticks usually don't make their presence immediately known, and can dig into a tender spot on your body (folds of skin and hairlines are favorites) and not be discovered for a day or two when the skin swelling and irritation finally reveal their residency. Don't try to pull a tick from your skin, as you will just break his neck and his head will remain in place, causing infection. It's better to hold something hot (a match or cigarette) near it, apply alcohol, kerosene, gasoline, or a strong tobacco solution. Such techniques will usually force the critter to back out pronto!

16

Ticks are particularly evident from April through July, and a body check after a day outdoors is a wise idea.

Mountain Sickness

This problem occurs when too rapid a gain to high elevation takes place. High altitude can be considered anywhere from above 5,280 feet, or one mile high. Colorado's average elevation is 6,800 feet, and three-quarters of our country's land above 10,000 feet lies in Colorado. More than half of Colorado lies above one mile high.

With higher elevation comes decreased oxygen and humidity content in the air. At 8,000 to 10,000 feet, there is approximately 40 to 50 percent less oxygen and about 50 to 80 percent less humidity available to the body when compared to sea level. Dehydration and lack of oxygen to the body, known as hypoxia, will cause symptoms of mountain sickness such as nausea, diarrhea, shortness of breath, insomnia, fast heartbeat, headache, nasal congestion, cough, increased flatulence, fatigue, and loss of appetite. To alleviate these symptoms, return to a lower elevation if possible. When first arriving at higher elevations, eat lightly, avoid alcohol, coffee, and sugar drinks, and keep physical exertion to a minimum. If you feel the effects of mountain sickness, stop and rest, breathe deeply, take nourishment from fruit juice or candy, and drink plenty of liquids.

It is estimated that up to one quarter of all visitors to Colorado feel the effects of mountain sickness.

Hyperventilation

Caused by too rapid breathing and decrease of the carbon dioxide level in the blood, hyperventilation results in lightheadedness and a chilled feeling. To treat, relax and breathe into a bag or hat until normal breathing is restored.

Giardiasis (gee-ar-dye-a-sis)

This serious disease is contracted by drinking untreated water containing the organism Giardia lamblia. The water can be very good smelling, looking, and tasting, and animals may drink from the same water. But while they are immune to the effects of the disease, you are not. Fortunately, the disease is curable when properly diagnosed and treated by a physician.

Symptoms: Diarrhea, little appetite, abdominal cramps, nausea, fever, increased gas, and bloating. Signs are not necessarily immediate. They may show up several days or even weeks after ingestion, and can last up to six weeks and recur over a period of many months.

Prevention: Boil water at least ten minutes. Boiling is more effective than chlorine or iodine water treatments, although these work well against most bacteria in water.

Hypothermia

This is the number one killer of outdoor recreationists. It is caused by exposure to cold and is aggravated by wetness, wind, and exhaustion. Cold reaches the brain, reasoning power is lost, and you are not aware of what is happening. You lose control of your hands, your internal temperature drops, and this leads to stupor, collapse, and finally death.

It is very important to stay dry. Choose rain gear that covers the neck, head, body, and legs. Most hypothermia cases occur between the temperatures of 30 and 50 degrees F., and sudden storms in summer in the mountains often produce these temperatures. In essence, you freeze to death even though the air temperature is above the freezing mark.

Symptoms: Slurred speech, uncontrollable shivering, incoherence, loss of memory, fumbling hands, problems with walking, drowsiness (to sleep is to die), exhaustion.

Treatment: Get the victim out of the wind and rain. Strip off all wet clothes and get the victim into warm, dry clothes and/or sleeping bag. Give the victim warm drinks but no alcohol. Keep the victim awake. Build a fire to keep the camp warm and get help as soon as possible.

Automobile Expectations

Due to elevation changes, your car may rebel and exhibit a lack of power, poor gas mileage, and sputtering. These are all symptoms of flooding, which means that the car isn't getting enough air—and that it is receiving too much gasoline. Vapor locks are very common in the mountains because the car is not tuned for the elevation. If necessary, see a mechanic to accomplish the proper adjustments.

As you drive up from sea level, your tire pressure can rise as much as ten pounds. Check your tires when they are cold, and keep the suggested pressure in them to avoid unnecessary wear.

You may notice the octane ratings of gasoline in the mountains to be less than at sea level. The reason is because gas burns hotter at high elevations, and if the octane wasn't adjusted to accommodate this fact, the heat could damage the valves.

When driving, use caution and drive defensively. There are many motorists on the roads who are not accustomed to driving in the mountains, and their skills aren't necessarily as sharp as they would be at home. When four-wheeling, check locally on road and weather conditions.

Plan your gas stops. Sometimes distances are further than they might look on the map, and there could be a lot of open space between filling stations. One more thing—at 10,000 feet, water boils at 194 degrees F. Make sure your cooling system is functioning properly!

Photography

With clean air, rugged mountains, narrow canyons, sparkling streams, abundant wildlife, colorful geology, and signs of snow year-round, Colorado offers even the most experienced photographer the opportunity and stimulus to take photographs.

Particularly for visitors who spend most of their time in less spectacular surroundings, the physical characteristics of Colorado will provide fuel for the fire in any shutter bug's eye. Because of the brightness of the sun's rays during midday, we'd suggest photos be shot in morning and evening to take advantage of the dramatic effect of shadows, light, and reflection. Don't leave home without your camera!

ARKANSAS RIVER

Map Reference 9 & 10

The length of the Arkansas River to be highlighted here is 117 miles, from the town of Leadville to Canon City. Due to toxic discharges into the river from abandoned mining operations in the gulches immediately adjacent to Leadville, the section of river from that point downstream to Twin Lakes must be rated mediocre during most of the year. During the spring and fall spawning migrations, this section of river can fish better due to increased fish populations moving upstream. Normally, however, river volumes are insufficient to dilute the toxins enough to encourage a quality fish and insect population. This entire section is fenced from the highway, but permission may be granted when requested. Below Twin Lakes, BLM (Bureau of Land Management) land is intermixed with private property, and permission should be obtained whenever doubts are present.

Unfortunately, there are times when the outflow from Turquoise Lake is so small that some places along the five-mile reach of the Lake Fork River are totally dry. This occurs when water is diverted from Turquoise to Twin Lakes. When water levels are adequate, fishing in the Lake Fork can be good. Permission should be obtained.

Below the Twin Lakes turnoff onto Highway 82, the first 3.5 miles is open access with no fences. Below this area, fences parallel the road, and if there is any question concerning private or public property, permission should be obtained. This part of the river, and all water downstream, should be considered big water, and careful wading is a must. Along the banks are chokecherry, mountain gooseberry, and alder. The riverbed contains a good number of granite boulders, and cleats and/or wading staff wouldn't be a bad idea.

Access to the river from the town of Buena Vista is very easy. Merely drive east on East Main Street, and you will arrive at a parking area next to the river. Fish here, or drive upstream along the river for about one-half mile. The river is fifty to sixty feet wide with long, deep runs, a lot of boulders, and plenty of pocket water. Another access is to turn north at the Colorado Highway Department garage in town, located at the corner of East Main Street and North Colorado Avenue. The road will then cross the river and parallel it for about a mile before reaching four rock tunnels bored through the side of the hill. Access is easily available along this reach, but beyond the tunnels it becomes more difficult, as the road leaves the river. Further upstream, the road does return to the river and goes to the Otero Pump Station. The river here averages about seventy feet in width.

Brown's Canyon at Hecla Junction is a take-out point for commercial rafting companies. It is also an access point for anglers. From the settlement of Nathrop, located eight miles south of Buena Vista, drive six miles south to a gravel road east of the highway. The sign reads, "Hecla Jct./Brown's Canyon." Follow the road 2.7 miles to the river, where you can wade either up or downstream. Most fishermen find the water upstream to be more appealing, and prefer to cross the river here and follow the railroad tracks up through the pink-hued granite and the ponderosa and pinon pine. Almost all of the canyon is on public land. Care should be taken crossing here, as the current can be deceptively strong at higher volumes. There have been stories of rattlesnakes living in this area of the canyon, but they are not a normal occurrence. Take precautions while fishing here, and your chances of sighting one will be very remote. Caution: Don't float privately through Brown's Canyon. It is too dangerous!

From Salida east to Texas Creek, the adjacency of the river and highway make access no problem. Some private property is mixed with public, but plenty of water is available to keep an angler casting for a long time. Long runs, sweeping bends, deep pools, and rocky ledges make the Arkansas an exciting river to fish. Brown trout are predominant and average about twelve inches. Below Texas Creek, the river tumbles through a canyon environment, while above it, it glides through flats and riffles. At the Texas Creek Trading Post, the sport flyfisherman may be granted permission by Ed Valdez to fish a mile and a half of the river that he controls behind his fly shop. His strict regulations assure continued improvement in the quality of the angling here.

A word of caution concerning safety and fishing success on the Arkansas—this river is subject to relatively sudden flow changes as Eastern Slope water demands change. From the fisherman's point of view, a volume of 200 to 500 cfs is most desirable. Demands for irrigation water, however, can bring the flow up to 4,000 cfs.

The Arkansas is primarily a brown trout river, but you can also expect to take some rainbows, especially during the day.

Insects

For the entire distance of the river, caddis flies are the primary trout food. Hatches can be expected from May through September, with literally millions of the small gray insects moving over the river in mating flights early in the season. Stoneflies and Mayflies are also abundant in the river, and both nymph and adult patterns are effective. The big Pteronarcys and Acroneuria nymphs should be fished in the riffles and where the riffles empty into slower runs and pools. In late summer, the Arkansas produces well to ants and hoppers fished up against the banks.

Tackle

As a river that can at times be considered somewhat substantial, we recommend using at least a six weight fly outfit under normal conditions. Occasionally, when the water is at minimum flow, five weight would be perfect. Most fishing will be done with floating lines, although at higher volumes, a sink-tip would be good for streamer fishing. Spin fishermen will want to use four- to six-pound test lines.

Flies and Lures

Dry Renegades and Grey Elk Hair Caddis with olive or gray bodies in size No. 14 are very popular, particularly in the evenings. Don't forget the old standbys of Adams, Humpies, and Irresistible. In the river down around Texas Creek, the Arkansas River Stonefly and Arkansas River Caddis are two local favorites.

Caddis Larvae and Pupae patterns work well, as do large black and brown stonefly nymphs from size 2 to 6. Other good nymphs include the Gold Ribbed Hare's Ear, Renegade, Woolly Worm, Girdle Bug, and Muskrat, these in sizes 12 to 18. Streamer flies should include Black or Tan Kiwi Muddlers, Zonkers, Little Rainbow Trout, and black Woolly Buggers.

Area Lakes

Turquoise Lake is located about three miles west of the town of Leadville and offers fishing and relaxing to a large number of people during the summer. This 1,500-acre fishery is populated primarily with brown trout, with other species available, including lake trout. Above the lake, hiking trails lead to high alpine lakes. From Harrison Street in town, turn west of 6th Street, and proceed to County Road 4, which goes to the dam. From Highway 24 in Stringtown next to Leadville, turn north at the blue sewer plant/Colorado Mountain College turnoff at the City Limit sign. From here, it is four miles to the lake.

Twin Lakes are most famous for their Mackinaw (lake trout), but are also well stocked with rainbows and cutthroats. Most of the fishing is from the shore, but boats are allowed, and trolling for the Macks offers the angler the opportunity to catch fish up to twenty pounds. This is also good water for belly-boating. Standard streamers work well, and a particular favorite is the White Zonker.

The Crystal Lakes are located 1.7 miles downstream from the intersection of State Highway 14 and the Turquoise Lake Road 300. As a public area supervised by the Forest Service, it is well signed, and parking space is available just off the highway. It is a fine place for the family to fish from the shore or from a personal boat for small trout, with the chance for one up to twenty inches in the deeper water in the middle of the lake. Evening will see the surface boiling with fish as they come up to small insects. Black patterns and Adams in size 16 seem to be consistently effective.

LEADVILLE

Whether you enjoy the historic atmosphere of Colorado mining days or the high country atmosphere of clear, thin air, Leadville has both in abundance. Located at an elevation of 10,152 feet at the headwaters of the Arkansas River, the "cloud city" boasts the world's highest golf course and the highest airport in North America. The 14,000-foot-plus mountain peaks to the west of town offer the visitor a truly spectacular view throughout the year. In the glacially formed Sawatch Range, Mount Elbert (Colorado's highest peak) at 14,433 feet and Mount Massive at 14,421 feet, present an unmatched horizon.

This famous silver mining center boasted a population estimated at 60,000 in the early 1880s. Nearly a billion dollars in minerals were taken from the mountains of this area, and some of those dollars were spent erecting several buildings, including the elegant Tabor Opera House, built by mining millionaire H.A.W. Tabor.

With a population of 4,000, Leadville caters to its summer tourists. From guided tours of the down-to-earth, 105-year-old opera house, to above-the-earth scenic air tours of America's highest mountain peaks, ghost towns, and abandoned silver mines, the Leadville area offers many activities of interest.

The mountains provide hiking opportunities, and the town offers tennis, opera, a children's park, and self-guided historical tours of the downtown area as well as of the mining district. A multimedia-wide screen presentation of Leadville's historic past is shown daily during the summer months. West of Leadville, at an elevation of 10,000 feet, the entire family can enjoy the operations of America's second oldest federal fish hatchery. The Leadville National Fish Hatchery features a nature trail of approximately one mile in length around

Evergreen Lakes, in addition to the opportunity to view many trout being raised at the hatchery.

Turquoise Lake, at 9,869 feet, is four miles west of Leadville and is one of the major attractions of the area. The lake is one of the water storage facilities for the Fryingpan-Arkansas transmountain water diversion project.

To the north of Leadville, on Tennessee Pass (10,424 feet), stands a memorial to honor the Tenth Mountain Division, which trained at nearby Camp Hale during World War II. From this point, access is available for hikers who wish to use Colorado Trail 1776. Regionally, it can be hiked from here thirty miles south to Twin Lakes, and another twenty-five miles south to Cottonwood Creek west of Buena Vista.

Twin Lakes are two glacially formed bodies of water that have been enlarged to provide additional water storage in the Fryingpan-Arkansas project. The forebay north of Twin Lakes receives water from Turquoise Lake by conduit. Turquoise Lake, in turn, receives water from the Frying Pan River drainage on the Western Slope.

Twin Lakes Village, listed in the National Register of Historic Places, was a major stage center during the mining days. Passengers arrived from Leadville in concord stages, transferred to canvas tops, and made their way over Independence Pass to the mining camps of Independence and Aspen.

Twelve miles north of Leadville on Colorado Highway 91 is the Climax Molybdenum Mine. This is the largest molybdenum mine in the world, and visitors are welcome.

Camping

This area offers several camping opportunities. North of town is the Tennessee Pass Campground with five units. To the south on Forest Road 110 is Halfmoon and Elbert campgrounds, with twenty-six units. These sites provide a base camping area for hikes to Mount Elbert and Mount Massive, the two highest points in Colorado. Just to the west of town on Turquoise Lake, three campgrounds are available with a total of 157 units. No hook-ups or showers are available at these lakeside sites, but commercial campgrounds in the area offer these services. A trail around the north side of the lake gives access to the Colorado Trail for anyone wishing to do some hiking.

Fifteen miles south of Leadville is the turnoff onto Highway 82 toward Twin Lakes and Independence Pass. Just beyond the village of Twin Lakes about three miles are two campgrounds, Twin Peaks and Parry Peak, with sixty-two units available along Lake Creek. Hikers find these campgrounds convenient, as they are close to the Colorado Trail going north to Tennessee Pass, and south to Cottonwood Creek.

Chamber of Commerce, Box 861, 809 Harrison Ave., Leadville 80461. Phone: 486-0418.

U.S. Forest Service, Box 970, 130 W. 5th Street. Phone: 486-0749.

Leadville

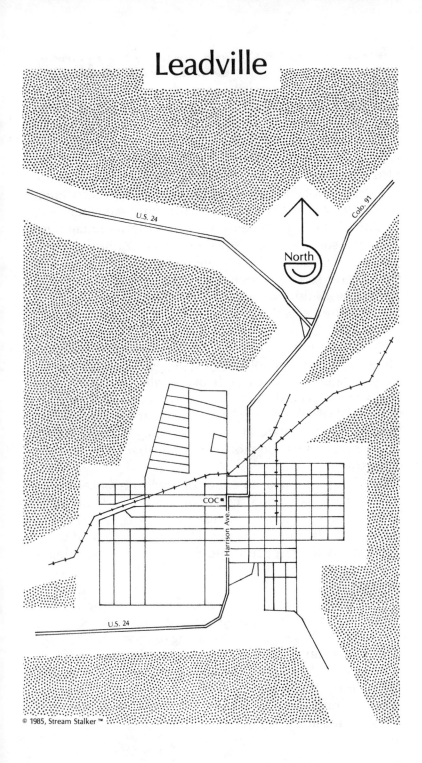

BUENA VISTA

Situated in the center of the state at 7,954 feet, Buena Vista (Spanish for "beautiful view") lies at the foot of the highest mountain region within the continental United States. Its main industries are tourism, ranching, and mining. Activity here centers around the mountain and historical surroundings. Nowhere in the country can you see so many of America's highest mountain peaks so closely and so concentrated. In the comfort of your car, you can easily drive to vantage points that offer unequalled views of the Collegiate Peaks of the Sawatch Range. Ten peaks over 14,000 feet are vividly in view for your enjoyment and your camera. Within thirty miles of each other lie three of the four highest peaks in the continental United States. On the east side of the valley rise the Buffalo Peaks to over 13,000 feet. The combination of these two ranges makes the Collegiate Valley one of the mildest climates in the state. It is called the "banana belt," receiving as much or more sunshine than anywhere in Colorado.

Amid this mountain splendor of the San Isabel National Forest lie 500 lakes and streams plus many ghost towns and historical sites. The ghost towns reflect the colorful mining and railroad history of the late 1800s when gold and silver made many a prospector into a millionaire. The mining towns of Romley, Hancock, and St. Elmo are major attractions here.

In Buena Vista, the entire family can enjoy hiking, swimming at the hot springs pool, going on mine tours, visiting the fish hatchery, and playing tennis and golf. River rafting with one of the commercial rafting companies is also popular. Although a small town of about 2,100, Buena Vista has thirteen churches, several fraternal organizations, and a paved 9,000-foot runway with servicing facilities.

Camping

Camping is popular in this area of exceptional natural beauty, historic mining camps, hiking trails, and fishing. Two campgrounds, Collegiate Peaks and Cottonwood Lake, are located west of Buena Vista on Highway 306. These have a total of fifty-seven units. A bit further south, west of Nathrop on Highway 162 along Chalk Creek, are Mount Princeton, Chalk Lake, Cascade, and Iron City campgrounds, with a total of sixty-three units. These areas fill early in the day at peak season, so don't wait too long to find your site.

Buena Vista Chamber of Commerce, P.O. Box P, Highway 24 South, Buena Vista 81211. Phone: 395-6612.

Police: 395-8654

Medical Clinic: 395-8632

U.S. Forest Service (in Salida): 539-3591

Buena Vista

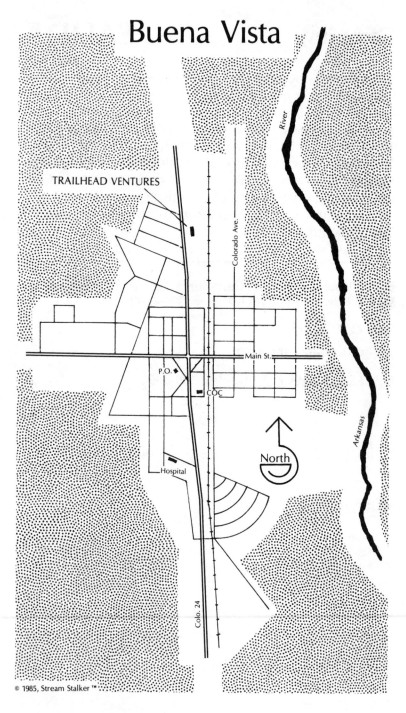

TRAILHEAD VENTURES

Colorado Ave.

Main St.

P.O.

COC

North

Hospital

Colo. 24

River

Arkansas

© 1985, Stream Stalker ™

SALIDA

Situated on the Arkansas River, the town of Salida is designated "The Heart of the Rockies." At an elevation of 7,036 feet, Salida, with a population of approximately 5,000, is primarily involved in the businesses of tourism, mining, and trade. From the 1880s, Salida (Spanish for "gateway") was a railroad center and supply town.

The 14,000-foot peaks to the west are a spectacular backdrop to the activities taking place here. The river is a focal point for rafting, fishing, and kayaking. The town annually hosts FIBARK (first in boating on the Arkansas), the longest whitewater kayak race in the world. The municipal nine-hole golf course is open from April through September.

Jeep tours to ghost towns, an aerial tramway allowing views of six mountain ranges, and horseback riding offer outdoor activities for the entire family. Salida Hot Springs provides three individual pools of mineral water for soaking or swimming, along with tennis courts and other recreational activities. Salida is also home to one of the country's largest trout hatcheries.

Camping

Southeast of Salida, you can camp at the Coaldale Campground three miles southwest of Coaldale on Forest Road 249. Seven tent sites here are located on Hayden Creek.

To the west and southwest of town, five campgrounds are available. The first is Angel of Shavano Campground, with seventeen units, located north of Highway 50 on Forest Service Road 214 along the North Fork of the Arkansas River. Six miles further on a narrow, rough road is

North Fork Reservoir Campground, with eight units.

Further west on Highway 50 is Garfield Campground, with eleven units, and yet further along the highway is Monarch Campground, with thirty-seven units.

O'Haver Lake Campground is located on Road 243. Turn west off Highway 285 five miles south of Poncha Springs and continue about three miles to the campground, with twenty-four units. The small reservoir here offers fishing, but no boating.

Salida Chamber of Commerce, 406 W. Rainbow Blvd. (Highway 50), Salida 81201. Phone: 539-2068.

U.S. Forest Service, Box 219, Salida. Phone: 539-3591.

Emergency: 539-6011.

Hospital: 539-6661 (B & lst St.)

Division of Game, Fish, and Parks: 539-6877.

Salida

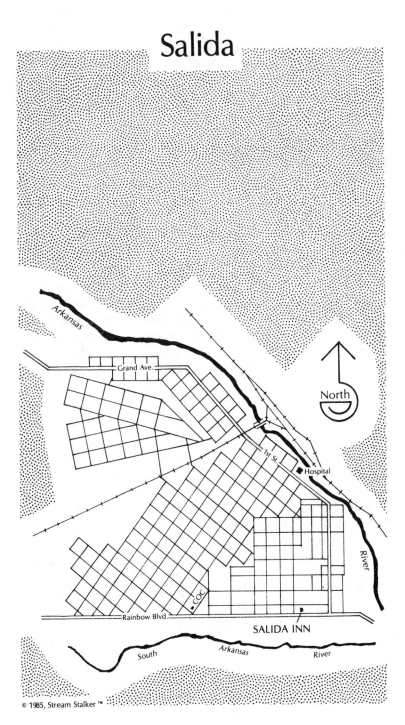

CANON CITY

Since Zebulon Pike explored this section of Colorado in 1806, the area close by has been a producer of oil, a livestock raising center, the home of the Colorado State Prison, and now a tourist center with the several attractions of the Royal Gorge.

The residents chose the Spanish spelling of "canyon" in 1859 because of its location near the "Grand Canon del Rio Arkansas."

The town was incorporated in 1872. Although the area has not exactly become the movie capital of the United States, as once it was thought to become when Tom Mix got his movie start here in 1910, it is one of the state's best locations because of its mild climate and proximity to scenic country. The town claims 355 days of sunshine per year.

As county seat of Fremont County, the metro area population is approximately 23,000 and is situated at 5,343 feet. A spectacular view of the Arkansas Valley can be gained from Skyline Drive, a narrow road sitting on a ridge just west of Canon City at an elevation of about 800 feet above the town.

At the Royal Gorge, the world's highest suspension bridge spans the distance of one-fourth mile over the Arkansas River, 1,055 feet below. Major tourist attractions are the world's steepest incline cable railway descending to the bottom of the gorge, the spectacular aerial tramway over the gorge, and the narrow gauge train ride along the rim.

Activities for visitors include three parks outside the city limits, plus six city parks. Several tennis courts are available, as is one public swimming pool, theatres, a bowling alley, nearby fishing in the Arkansas River, and horseback riding.

The town is served by daily bus service, and Fremont

County Airport is located seven miles east of the city with a 5,414-foot asphalt, lighted runway. Commercial air service is available at Colorado Springs and Pueblo.

Camping

Campgrounds are not situated within close proximity to town, but we list three that are available in the area.

Oak Creek Campground: This campground is located sixteen miles south of town on County Road 143. Trailers are not recommended due to sharp curves and steep grades. Seven units are available here for picnics or tent camping. There are toilets, but no drinking water. Use is light during the summer.

Lake Creek Campground: This campground is eleven miles south of Texas Creek on State Highway 69 to the village of Hillside, then three miles west on Forest Road 300. Fifteen units are available with toilets but no drinking water. This campground receives moderate use.

Alvarado Campground: Proceed twenty-five miles west of Canon City on Highway 50, then turn south twenty-five miles to Westcliffe, and finally ten miles west of Westcliffe to the campground. With forty-four units, toilets, and drinking water, this campground receives heavy use. It may be noisy at times from trail bikes in the area.

Chamber of Commerce, Box 366, Canon City 81212. Phone: 275-2331.

U.S. Forest Service, 248 Dozier St., Canon City. Phone: 275-1626.

Cañon City

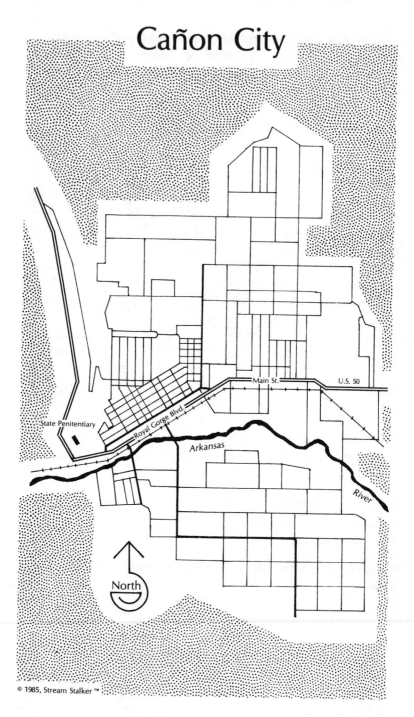

State Penitentiary

Royal Gorge Blvd.

Main St.

U.S. 50

Arkansas

River

North

© 1985, Stream Stalker ™

38

Buena Vista

Salida

Cañon City

BLUE RIVER

Map Reference 11

The Blue River from Dillon Dam to Kremmling flows north for thirty-six miles. On the west side of the valley, the wild and rugged peaks of the Gore Wilderness thrust majestically skyward, while to the east the valley sweeps more gently to the Williams Fork Mountains. At Green Mountain Reservoir, the valley is open, and trees of any size are scarce. The land is primarily sagebrush flats rising to the mountains in both directions. If wind were to blow, it would blow unresisted.

Between Dillon and Green Mountain you can expect the fish to average about eleven inches in length, with sixteen inches considered a good fish. A four-pounder here would be about the best you could expect. You will catch both browns and rainbows in the Blue, but the browns will predominate. Fishing pressure during the summer is fairly heavy.

The river is about sixty feet across, and wading is not difficult, but waders and felt soles are suggested. The river usually flows at between 200 and 800 cfs but is fished best at 200 to 300 cfs. Crossing at normal flows does not present a problem, with average depth about three feet. Water flows do fluctuate, however, due to the demands of the Denver Water Board, which uses this stored water for needs of the Eastern Slope.

Fishing is available sporadically along the entire length between Dillon and Green Mountain, with private and public water mixed. Most of the water open to the public is not fenced, so access is obvious. Parking along the highway presents no problem. There are no resorts along the river, but camping is available in the area (see Summit County information).

At Green Mountain Dam is a residential settlement of about twenty homes. You can walk through this area and fish the river for about two miles downstream of the dam. Downstream of the reservoir, near the confluence of the Blue and the Colorado rivers, the Trough Road intersects Highway 9 from the west. Following this road for about one mile fishing is available with permission only, under strict rules of the ranch owner who demands at the very least that anglers fish with flies. Fishing this entire area below the reservoir is best done with nymphs and streamers.

The river above Dillon Reservoir also provides fishing for a short distance, but due to the size of the stream here, flyfishing is most effective. The stream averages about twenty feet in width and can be good for rainbows and browns. Public fishing is available from the inlet upstream approximately two and one-half miles to the highway bridge. From here to Breckenridge, the river flows through private property. Because brown trout move into this section of river to spawn in the fall, it is closed to fishing from October 31 through January 31.

Insects

The insect populations on the river show no predominant families, so choices of artificials are fairly liberal. The hatches of Mayflies and caddis are steady throughout the summer, and periodic stonefly hatches prompt their use as adults, but more commonly as nymphs. Mayflies are most common in sizes 14 and 16, as are black, tan, and olive caddis adults. Stonefly imitations here do not run as large as on many rivers, with sizes 8 to 12 being common.

Tackle

In fly gear, size 5 and 6 outfits are all that you need. The river is small enough that sinking lines are not necessary. Spin fishermen will want to use two- to four-pound test lines.

Flies and Lures

Green Drakes and Blue Winged Olives in size 12 and 14, Elk Hair Caddis olive, tan or black bodies in 14s and 16s, Adams, Humpies, Grey Wulff, Royal Wulff also in 14s and 16s.

Nymphs—Zug Bug, Hare's Ear in 14s to 18s, Perla Stone, Mono Stone in No. 12, Brown Hackle Peacock in 12s to 16s. In larger patterns, try Hornbergs, Woolly Buggers, leech patterns, Spruce Fly, Zonker, and Matukas.

Terrestrials—Beetles occasionally and hopper patterns in August.

Lures—Small Rooster Tails, Mepps, and Panther Martins.

Dillon Reservoir

"Lake Dillon" is the largest body of water in central Colorado and literally covers the old mining town of Dillon. It has twenty-five miles of shoreline and contains rainbows, brook trout, browns, and kokanee salmon. Coho salmon have recently been stocked, and we suggest that these all be released so they have an opportunity to take hold and grow to maturity.

Ice-out on the lake is usually between May 15 and June 10. The two to three weeks immediately following ice-out are usually very good fishing until the lake turns over. An effective manner in which to fish the lake is from a boat or belly-boat working the inlets and bays. Lures suggested include 1½ to 3½ inch Rapalas, Mepps, Panther Martins, and Krocodiles. Fly patterns include Scuds, Fairy Shrimp, Grizzly Shrimp, wet Renegades in size 10 to 14, Grey Ugly in size 8 to 12, and Zonkers and Matukas in size 2 to 8.

Green Mountain Reservoir

Located twenty miles north of Silverthorne on Colorado Highway 9, this water contains browns, rainbows, and a strong population of kokanee salmon. Lake trout to fifteen pounds are also taken. This reservoir is not well suited to belly-boating because it is a deep lake that is exposed to the wind. The inlet area is open to the public and is a popular area to fish. Standard fly patterns are effective, and the Zonker works particularly well. Lures that seem most effective include the Kastmaster in ¼ and ⅜ oz. and the Krocodile from ⅛ to ⅜ oz.

SUMMIT COUNTY

The term "Summit County" refers to the communities of Silverthorne, Dillon, Frisco, Breckenridge, and Copper Mountain. The entire area was originally developed because of the mineral deposits in the surrounding mountains. It is now a summer and winter center for outdoor activities.

The first gold strike in the Blue River Valley occurred in 1859. Evidence of the ensuing mining activity is still apparent along the upper Blue River. Breckenridge was Colorado's first permanent Western Slope community. Within Summit County, more than sixty towns and mining camps developed. Most did not thrive after the mid-1890s due to lack of sufficient profitable minerals.

DILLON: On the east shore of Lake Dillon, this small community offers panoramic views of the Ten Mile Range, as well as easy access to the Blue River Valley. The town has a shopping center, golf, tennis, sailing, fishing, and cycling, offering the visitor plenty to do.

BRECKENRIDGE: This community is a beautiful Victorian town at the base of the Breckenridge ski area. In 1985, Breckenridge will boast the opening of its new eighteen-hole golf course. Breckenridge conducts its Music Institute in July, a camp for junior and senior high students.

FRISCO: This is the largest town in Summit County. Located on the western shore of Dillon Reservoir, the population is over 1,500. With a wide variety of lodging and shops, Frisco is the center of paved bike paths connecting the communities within the valley to nearby Vail.

The entire area is off of I-70, sixty-five miles west of Denver.

Camping

Camping in Summit County is concentrated around Lake Dillon and Green Mountain Reservoir. Seven campgrounds are located around Lake Dillon. One is for group camping, one is for hikers and bicyclists, and one is on an island with boat access only. This leaves four areas for the typical visitor. Together, they provide 360 campsites with toilets, drinking water, trailer spaces, trailer dump stations, and some with boat launching facilities.

To the north of Silverthorne on Highway 9 lies Green Mountain Reservoir, around which you can find six camping areas. They are mostly undeveloped, accommodate trailers, have toilets, and three of the six have drinking water. All of these sites are located between sixteen and twenty-eight miles from Silverthorne.

Four other campgrounds are available in the Summit County area. Rainbow Lakes Campground is 1.4 miles south of Frisco and Bakers Tank is 4.2 miles south of Frisco. To the north, along Highway 9, are Blue River Campground (7.8 miles from Silverthorne) and Cataract Creek, sixteen miles north.

For additional information on the many camping possibilities in this area, talk to the Summit County Chamber of Commerce or the U.S. Forest Service.

Breckenridge Medical Center: 453-6934.

Dillon Health & Treatment Center: 468-5344.

Summit County Clinic: 468-2478.

Summit County Medical Center: 668-3300.

Ambulance: 911.

Summit County Chamber of Commerce
P.O. Box 214, Frisco 80443

Dillon Ranger District, 101 W. Main, Drawer O, Frisco 80443. Phone: 668-5404.

Breckenridge

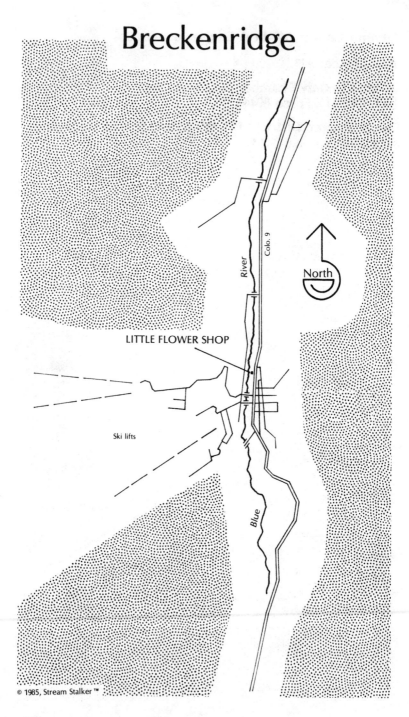

North

Colo. 9

River

LITTLE FLOWER SHOP

Ski lifts

Blue

Frisco

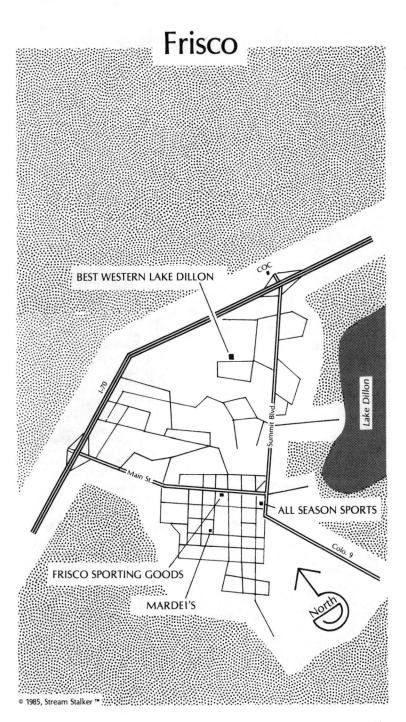

BEST WESTERN LAKE DILLON

COC

Lake Dillon

I-70

Summit Blvd.

Main St.

ALL SEASON SPORTS

Colo. 9

FRISCO SPORTING GOODS

MARDEI'S

North

© 1985, Stream Stalker ™

Dillon-Silverthorne

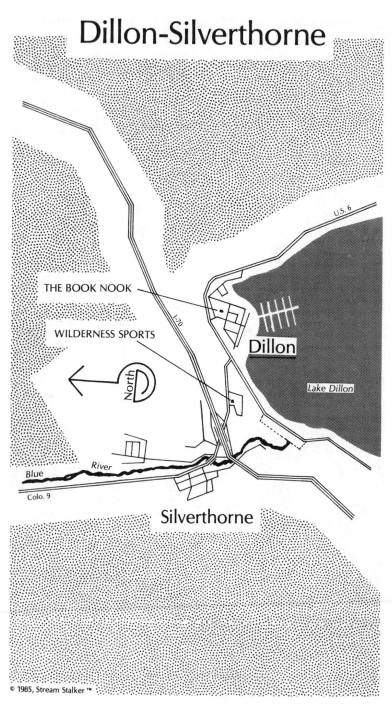

THE BOOK NOOK

WILDERNESS SPORTS

North

I-70

U.S. 6

Dillon

Lake Dillon

Blue River

Colo. 9

Silverthorne

© 1985, Stream Stalker ™

Breckenridge

Frisco

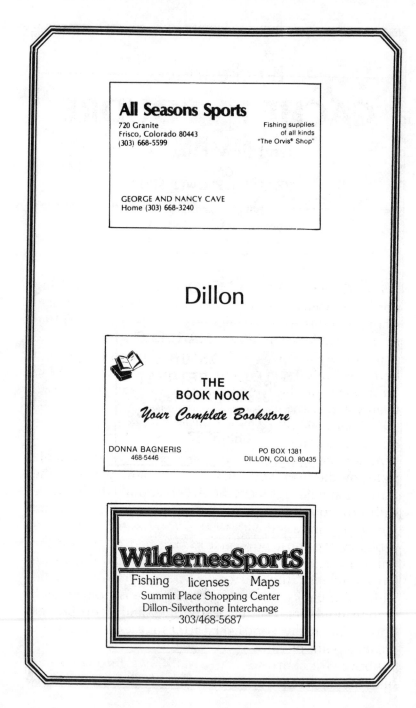

CACHE LA POUDRE RIVER

Map Reference 12

The Cache la Poudre River is reached by driving northwest from Fort Collins almost ten miles to Ted's Place, where you turn west on Highway 14. First sighting of the river is 1.4 miles from Ted's. At 2.8 miles, stop at the intake structure of the Poudre Valley Canal. The informative sign here gives information about the three stretches of Wild Trout water on the river, located at approximately three, twenty-eight, and thirty-eight miles from Ted's. At least these mileages will put you within the boundaries of the designated water.

Along the approximately forty-five miles of fishable water on the river, you will find much variety. Below The Narrows at mile eighteen, the river is about sixty feet wide with riffle/pool sequences, deep holes, slow bends, and long runs contrasted with some pocket water. This area is probably the most popular to fishermen of any on the entire river. Around mile twelve, the river is filled with large boulders. The Narrows contains very rough water with steep banks, and the riverbed here is clogged with granite boulders, causing fast chutes and deep plunge pools. This really is not very appealing water from the angler's point of view.

Above The Narrows, the river flows through steep hillsides, so watch for rocks on the highway, especially after a heavy rain. Below the State Fish Hatchery at mile thirty-nine, the water flows in smooth runs typical of a meadow stream. This is delightful water in the evenings with dry flies.

Because of the easy accessibility to the Poudre for so much of its length, and being close to a fairly large community, the river does receive considerable pressure, not only from anglers, but also from whitewater rafters and kayakers, as some areas of the river are well suited to these activities. For this reason, we strongly recommend a catch and release philosophy to allow more than one angler to feel the enjoyment of landing those fish that are relatively wild and larger than the "catchables" stocked by the state. Streams like this, that receive heavy fishing pressure, deserve a more thoughtful and sportsmanlike approach to the sport we all enjoy so much.

The fish population of the Poudre is split fairly evenly between the predominant brown and the rainbow trout, with a larger percentage of cutthroats in the upper river. Above The Narrows, you will also hook a good percentage of Rocky Mountain whitefish. The average size of the fish throughout the river is about eleven inches, with one of sixteen inches considered to be a good fish. In most Rocky Mountain streams, a fish of this size is probably five years old. What a shame to kill a fish that has survived this long, depriving another angler the opportunity to fish for it!

Wading the river normally is not a problem, but we do suggest using felt-soled chest waders. They will help you keep your balance a bit better as you watch the occasional bald eagle or golden eagle soar in the canyon thermals or catch a glimpse of the big horn sheep herd in the upper valley. Also keep your eyes open for the occasional rattlesnake that could be spotted along the lower river.

As with most Colorado rivers, you will enjoy pleasant fishing in March and April before the runoff gets underway, and then again after July 4 as the summer season sets in.

This is predominantly a caddis fly river, with large populations of Hydropsyche, Rhyacophila, and

Brachycentrus. A variety of subaquatic and adult imitations should be carried when fishing here. There is also a substantial number of midges on which the trout feed regularly. The mayflies are represented primarily by Baetis and Ephemerella, but are not present in the quantity seen in the caddis. Bring along some imitations of grandis and doddsi in size 12 for those special moments when these two large insects are on the water. The most important stonefly is represented by a golden stone nymph pattern in sizes 8 to 12. Hoppers are good in small sizes (12 to 14) in June during a dry year, and then again in late August through September using sizes 6 to 8.

Tackle

For the flyfisherman, a five weight here is perfect with a floating line. Spin fishermen prefer two and four pound lines. There are not active guide services in this area to our knowledge, but information can be obtained at local tackle shops.

Flies and Lures

Dries—Adams, Colorado King, and Elk Hair Caddis in Nos. 14-18. Also Renegade, Red Quill, and Royal Humpy in those same sizes. Rusty Spinner in Nos. 16 and 18, with midge patterns in sizes 18-22.

Nymphs—Best is a Golden Stone in sizes 8-12. Also Olive Caddis Larvae Nos. 12-16, Gold Ribbed Hare's Ear in Nos. 10-18, and Breadcrust in Nos. 10-16.

Streamers—Muddlers in sizes 8-12, Zonkers in No. 8, and Black Woolly Buggers in Nos. 8-12.

Lures—Mepps and Panther Martin.

FORT COLLINS

Fort Collins is the center of business, education, tourism, recreation, and medicine for the entire area near the Poudre River. The city is one of the fastest growing in the country, with a current population of approximately 80,000 and a projected growth to 150,000 by the year 2000.

As a university town, the community benefits in many ways from the influence of the 18,000-student Colorado State University. The Lincoln Center is home to many organizations in the performing arts, including symphony, theatre, and ballet. The university employs almost 7,000 residents, making it the largest employer in Larimer County.

Light industry, exemplified by Eastman Kodak Company and Hewlett-Packard, are drawn to Fort Collins for many reasons, including its favorable four-season climate. At an elevation of 5,000 feet, the weather is generally predictable, with extreme weather the exception.

The city offers the visitor a wide variety of normal amenities, and in addition is a base of operations for trips into the nearby mountains.

Fishing in the Poudre River, Red Feather Lakes, and Horsetooth Reservoir is convenient and nearby, as is the spectacular Rocky Mountain National Park. Horsetooth also offers boating, water skiing, and swimming.

Lory State Park is located adjacent to the west shore of Horsetooth Reservoir. It contains 2,600 acres in the foothills with very interesting rock formations of red sandstone, and offers a spectacular view of Fort Collins. Under the control of the Colorado Division of Parks and Recreation, the area has six backcountry campsites, but no vehicular camping. There are also twenty-two miles of hiking trails in the area.

Lodging and restaurants are available in abundance

throughout the city, and for private plane operators, the municipal airport has a 6,500-foot lighted runway that will accommodate aircraft to and including 727 jets.

Services are conducted in approximately seventy churches, golf is played at four courses, and the community swimming pool is open to the public. Also available are tennis courts, two roller skating rinks, the Fort Collins Museum, and a city park.

Fishing in the Poudre (pronounced "poo-der") River starts nine miles northwest of town at the start of what is known as "Colorado's Trout Route."

Camping

Several campgrounds are available as you drive west on Highway 14 following the Poudre River. Using Ted's Place as the zero reading on your odometer, there are three main sites within the first twenty-five miles. They are Ansel Watrous Campground, Narrows Campground, and Mountain Park Campground, with a total of seventy-four units. The latter is the largest with forty-three units, hiking trails, drinking water, toilets, and trailer parking.

Another three major areas are upstream to mile forty-five. They include Kelly Flats, Big Bend, and Sleeping Elephant, with a total of fifty units.

During July and August, you should try to secure a site early in the day to have a good choice of locations.

Fort Collins Chamber of Commerce, 225 So. Meldrum St., Fort Collins 80522. Phone: 482-3746.

Arapaho and Roosevelt National Forests, 240 W. Prospect, Fort Collins 80526. Phone: 224-1100.

Colorado Division of Parks and Outdoor Recreation, 3842 So. Mason, Fort Collins 80525. Phone: 226-6641.

Lory State Park, 708 Lodgepole Drive, Bellvue 80512. Phone: 493-1623.

Fort Collins

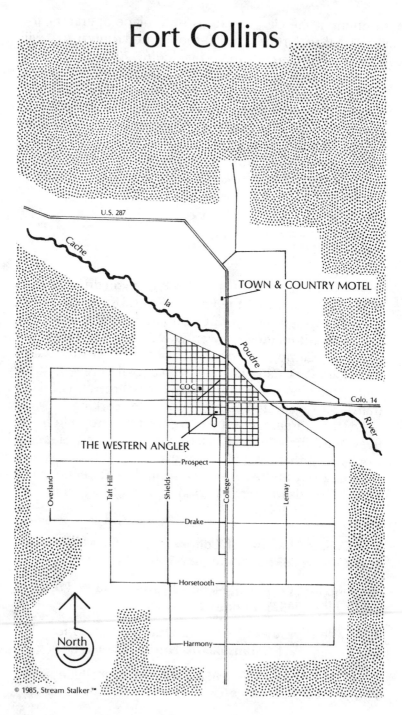

U.S. 287

Cache

la

Poudre

TOWN & COUNTRY MOTEL

COC

Colo. 14

River

THE WESTERN ANGLER

Prospect

Overland

Taft Hill

Shields

College

Lemay

Drake

Horsetooth

North

Harmony

© 1985, Stream Stalker ™

Fort Collins

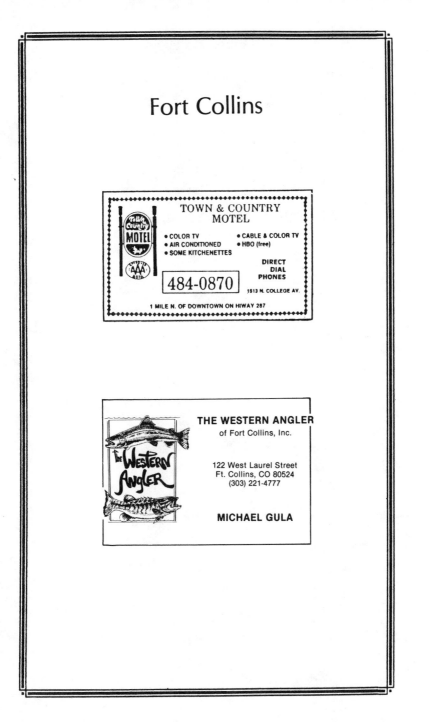

River Notes

COCHETOPA CREEK

Map Reference 1

To find this Wild Trout water, set your odometer at 0.0 at the east edge of the town of Gunnison and travel east on Highway 50 until you arrive at the intersection of Highway 114 at mile 7.7. Turn south on 114 and you will start to climb the gently rolling hills of this ranch country for about six miles, where you will enter into a rather narrow canyon. Access to the creek begins at about twenty-one miles, where a picnic area is located next to the creek, which is about fifteen feet wide. The creek is narrow and winding, and the banks are thick with willows and mountain alder.

At mile twenty-five, the canyon opens into a wide valley, where the stream starts to meander through open sagebrush country. This area is fenced and is private. At mile twenty-eight, you will turn onto Road NN14, a gravel road toward Old Agency. At 30.3 miles, you will notice a series of signs indicating that there is access to the Wild Trout water beyond the fence. This is a catch and release area only through a broad open valley without even willows to help break the wind. At mile 31.2, turn right onto Road KK14, again to Old Agency. There is lease water in this section with an access lane going off to the right at mile 32.0.

Although the creek is small, it does produce trout in the ten- to twelve-inch range, with larger fish sometimes taken from under the cutbanks on large streamer patterns.

The word Cochetopa is an Indian term meaning "Pass of the Buffalo." You probably won't sight any buffalo as you fish this stream, but you should see some rainbow trout, brooks, and cutthroat.

If you continue on NN14 for 2.3 miles past the KK14 intersection, you will arrive at Dome Reservoirs. These two impoundments are easily fished from the shore and sometimes produce a good brook trout in addition to cutthroat and rainbow.

For all of the fishing here, standard patterns work well both in nymphs and dry flies, with large streamers effective at times for bigger fish under the banks.

COLORADO RIVER

The Colorado River, as it flows through the large cattle and hay ranches of its upper reaches, is a perfect example of a fine fishery designated as Gold Medal water, yet offers a very limited angling opportunity to the public. Of the approximately thirty miles of river from Granby Reservoir down to Kremmling, which is paralleled by U.S. Highway 40, all of the river except about five miles flows through ranches where permission to fish is rarely granted. Several of these ranchers have leased their property to angling clubs, which of course are totally off-limits to fishing except to members and invited guests. A few licensed outfitters in the area also have permission to access some parcels of property along the river, as well as float specified stretches.

One of the areas open to public fishing is the two miles through Byer's Canyon located between Parshall and Hot Sulphur Springs. This stretch of river is about fifty feet wide and bounces through a boulder-filled channel about fifty feet below the highway. Parking is available along the road, and the access to the river is up and down the steep embankment. Because of the loose rocks and gravel of this bank, extra caution should be used to avoid sliding into the river. This area of the river is truly pocket water with only short pools and runs between the rocks. Railroad tracks parallel the river through the canyon, making the walk between pools somewhat easier than walking the riverbank. In addition to the canyon water, there is a short stretch of state property just below the canyon that is open to the public. This water is at the Lone Buck State Wildlife Area below the highway bridge.

Another very short piece of river open to anglers is located just below the town of Parshall. There is no fence here, and from the highway, an island is visible in the river. It is private and posted, but the river downstream is open for a short distance. There is also a short section just east of Kremmling. The Wild Trout water below Kremmling in Gore Canyon is inaccessible by vehicle and requires hiking to the river or floating it.

Because of so much water closed to the public and the open water being fished essentially by sport fishermen, the size of fish in the Colorado tends to be larger than in more pressured rivers with nonprotective regulations. With a good mix of rainbows and browns, the average size is about thirteen inches. It is also nice to know that when you have a strike, it is from a trout, as there are no whitefish in the river.

Until 1921, the Colorado River above its confluence with the Green River was called the Grand River. We suggest wearing chest waders to permit good mobility.

Fraser River

Map Reference 4

The Fraser River flows from its headwaters in Arapaho National Forest south of Winter Park through Middle Park and Fraser Canyon to its confluence with the Colorado River west of Granby. About sixteen miles of river in Fraser Canyon between Tabernash and Granby presently have Wild Trout status. The only access is by hiking from either end of this section along the Denver and Rio Grande Railroad right-of-way. Fishermen wishing to test this section of river should make certain they have permission.

Tackle

A six weight is adequate on this river, with floating lines and twelve-foot leaders. If you fish the lakes in the area, you might wish to use a fast sinking or lead core line to get down to the fish.

Flies and Lures

Dries—Small grey caddis imitations work well. Elk Hair Caddis Nos. 14 to 18 is good, as is a local Grey Parachute Caddis in Nos. 16 and 18. The Royal Wulff and Royal Humpy are good attractors in No. 13, and the grasshopper imitations are good in August.

Nymphs and Wets—Renegade, Western Coachman, Rio Grande King, Hare's Ear, Zug Bug good in Nos. 12-16. For bigger flies, use brown and black stonefly nymphs, Woolly Worms, and Brown Hackle Peacock in Nos. 2 to 6. A tan or golden stone nymph in size 12 can be good.

Lures—Favorites include Swiss-Swing, Mepps, Rapalas, and Panther Martin.

Lakes

Many visitors to this part of the state take advantage of the fishing opportunities available at the very source of the Colorado River. The so-called Great Lakes of the Rockies give birth to this river, and fishing possibilities abound in Grand Lake, Shadow Mountain Reservoir, and Granby Reservoir. Fishing here is done from boat and shore—in about equal proportion. Although most fish caught are brown, brook, and rainbow trout, kokanee salmon thrive here and provide a large part of the catch. The main attraction to boat fishermen is the lake trout. Most of these large (up to twenty-five pounds) fish are taken by casting or trolling from a boat, but some are caught each year by flyfishermen. Boats and tackle are available for rent at the marinas.

The best areas for the flyfisherman are at the lake inlets—two into Grand Lake, four into Granby Reservoir, and the only tributary into Shadow Mountain is the North Fork of the Colorado River.

Special trolling gear is used here for the lake trout, along with Daredevles and large spinners. The flyfisherman can use large streamers with success. A Zonker about four inches long is a good lake trout pattern.

GRAND LAKE

The town and the lake have the same name. Earliest history of the area dates to the early 1800s, when it was used by the Utes, Arapahoe, and Cheyenne Indians. The town itself was originally platted in 1881. Story has it that during a battle between the Utes and Cheyennes, the Ute braves loaded their women and children onto rafts and pushed them into Grand Lake for safety. Winds picked up, the rafts capsized, and all were lost. The lake was then considered evil, and early morning eerie mists and sounds heard across the lake are thought to be the spirits of the dead. The lake is also referred to sometimes as Spirit Lake.

The town, at 8,369 feet, is very tourist-oriented, yet is very low key in its commercial appearance. No multistoried buildings here—just a small-town flavor popular with tourists wishing to relax in a casual environment. This resort is literally nestled in the lodgepole forest, and some of the lodges are almost hidden from view due to the trees. Many activities are available, including tennis, golf on the nation's highest eighteen-hole course with grass greens, live theatre in the round, rodeos, hot air balloon races and rides, rafting, wind surfing, hiking, fishing, and horseback riding.

The western entrance to Rocky Mountain National Park is one mile north of town. This, of course, is the western end of Trail Ridge Road, the highest (12,000 feet) continuous paved highway in North America. This road follows an old Ute trail along the top of a ridge through an environment of arctic tundra. Open from late May into October, the artery offers fifty miles of spectacular valleys, glaciers, and mountains. The park has elevations to 14,256 feet, and the highway terminates at its eastern end at Estes Park. In addition to the great scenery, it isn't uncommon to sight wildlife, both big and small game, as you travel this road.

Referred to as the Great Lakes of the Rockies, the area between the towns of Grand Lake and Granby boast three separate lakes with a total recreational shoreline of 150 miles. The first is Grand Lake, the largest natural body of water in Colorado. Immediately to the south is Shadow Mountain Lake, and one more mile south rests the manmade Lake Granby. With this much water close at hand, fishing, boating, and sailing are prominent summer pastimes. Plenty of boat rentals are available at the adjacent marinas for water skiing, fishing, or just relaxing on one of the lakes.

Lake Granby and Shadow Mountain Lake store water to be transported to the Eastern Slope through the mountains via the Alva B. Adams tunnel. The outlet stream from Grand Lake is considered the beginning of the Colorado River. A word of caution to boaters—sudden storms can occur over the lakes, making boating dangerous due to strong winds and high waves. Small boat operators should be watchful of possible approaching storms and act accordingly.

Other summer activities include historic tours, boat parades, regattas, Yacht Club races, golf tournaments, plus many special events.

Camping

Camping sites are plentiful between the towns of Grand Lake and Granby, and should one area be filled, other options are available.

Greenridge Campground: Drive 2.5 miles south of town to County Road 66. Turn east and continue 1.5 miles to the campground located on the south end of Shadow Mountain Lake. You will find eighty-three sites with tables and fire grates. Drinking water, toilets, a trailer dump station, and a boat launch are available.

Stillwater Campground: Located 5.9 miles south of Grand Lake on Highway 34. Available are 148 sites with tables, fire grates, toilets, and drinking water. There is also a trailer dump station.

See the Granby write-up for additional campgrounds in the area.

Sheriff: 727-8244.

Three Lakes Medical Center: 627-3481.

Grand Lake Ambulance: 627-3311.

Chamber of Commerce, Box 57, Grand Lake 80447. Phone: 627-3402.

Grand Lake

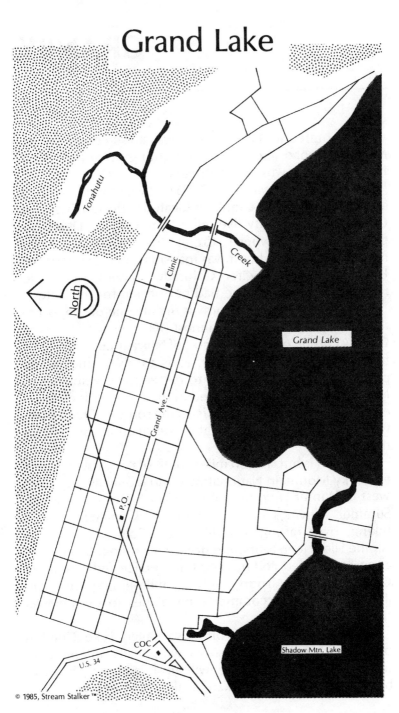

© 1985, Stream Stalker ™

GRANBY

Incorporated in 1906, Granby was a rail center on the Moffat Railroad and was the freighting point for Grand Lake and the towns in North Park.

Located at an elevation of 7,935 feet with a population of approximately 1,100, Granby is located in the ranch land of Grand County, eighty-five miles from Denver. Due to its proximity to Strawberry Creek, the town was almost named Strawberry, but it was instead named to honor the U.S. district attorney for Colorado, Granby Hillyer, to recognize the services he had performed for the state.

Granby's business economy is mainly one of support to the area's ranches. With almost 100 ranches in Grand County cutting over 40,000 acres of hay, agriculture is basic to the income of the town, as is tourism, due to the proximity of the community to recreation possibilities in Middle Park. Granby is located in the crossroads of travel east-west in Middle Park and is on the route to Grand Lake, which is a very popular vacation destination throughout the summer.

The town is but sixteen miles south of the west entrance to Rocky Mountain National Park and is only twenty miles west of Winter Park, one of Colorado's famous ski areas. Summer activities out of Winter Park include tennis, hiking, river rafting, chairlift rides, Colorado's longest Alpine Slide, jeep tours, and horseback riding. Granby has a regularly scheduled bus and train service and is near the Grand County Airport, with its mile-long paved and lighted runway, accommodating planes to business jet size.

Nearby Granby Reservoir (also called Lake Granby) provides recreation to visitors with many interests. In particular, fishermen here will find rainbows, browns, brook trout, cutthroat, kokanee salmon, silver salmon, and

Mackinaw (lake trout). In addition to fishing, the area offers rafting, boating, stables, and two golf courses.

Camping

Several camping sites are available to the north and south of town. Campers wishing to stay in the lake region north of Granby can use Willow Creek or Arapaho Bay campgrounds. Willow Creek is found by driving north of town 5.3 miles on Highway 34, and turning west on County Road 40. Proceed 3.5 miles to the campground on Willow Creek Reservoir. Here you will find thirty-five sites for tents and trailers, with drinking water and toilets. This is a quiet, isolated area with a boat launch and fishing.

To reach Arapaho Bay Campground, drive north 5.4 miles on Highway 34 to County Road 6. Turn east and drive 8.6 miles to the camping area. This road is blacktop for one mile, and the balance is gravel. Seventy-seven sites are available here with tables, fire grates, drinking water, and toilets. You will also find hiking trailheads and a boat launch on Granby Reservoir.

To the north of Granby on Highway 125 is Sawmill Gulch Campground, with five sites. Toilets are available, but no drinking water. There is also no fee. Beyond Sawmill another 2.2 miles is Denver Creek Campground with twenty-two sites. Again, toilets are available, but there is no drinking water, and no fee is required. Both are adjacent to Willow Creek and receive moderate use.

Another campground, located south of Granby, is Tabernash Campground, on Highway 40, 5.5 miles from town. Here you will find thirty sites with toilets, but no drinking water. No fee is required, and the campground receives only moderate use.

Chamber of Commerce: 200 E. Agate Ave., Granby 80446. Phone: 887-2311.

Granby Medical Clinic: 201 E. Jasper. Phone: 887-2117.

Timberline Medical Clinic, 62801 U.S. Highway 40. Phone: 887-2108.

U.S. Forest Service, Jct. Highways 43 and 40, Granby. Phone: 887-3331.

Sheriff: 887-3866.

River Notes

Granby

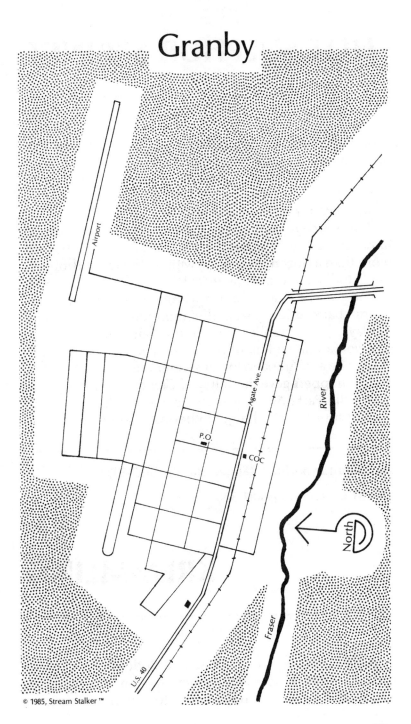

© 1985, Stream Stalker ™

73

HOT SULPHUR SPRINGS

Famous in 1885 for its soothing vapor waters, this site had been giving therapy to miners and lumbermen since it was founded in 1861 by William Byers, founder of the *Rocky Mountain News*, published in Denver. It is today the county seat for Grand County.

In those days of the late 1880s, the town had several hundred residents during the summer months, but no more than a dozen during the winter. The locals dropped the "Hot" from the name in 1894, but restored it in 1912.

Home of the Grand County Museum with local artifacts dating back 8,500 years, the museum contains many displays, photographs, manuscripts, and buildings that give you a real feeling of pioneer life in the 1800s.

The Ute and Arapaho Indians summered here where the French trappers gave the valley of Grand County the name of Middle Park. As in days past, current industry centers around tourism, ranching, lumbering, and mining.

Hot Sulphur Springs Ranger Station: 887-3301.

Sheriff (in Granby): 887-3866.

KREMMLING

In 1884, a Dillon merchant named Rudolph Kremmling opened a branch store at the junction of the roads leading east to Hot Sulphur Springs, south to Dillon, and west to

Steamboat Springs, and since that time the site has borne his name (except for the years 1891 to 1895, when it was called Kinsey City after the Kinsey brothers, who platted the town).

To the French fur trappers in the valley in 1820, the word "park" meant enclosure. The area surrounding Kremmling was named Old Park, since it was a flat plain surrounded by mountains. This reference gave way to the name Middle Park, which is the name used today. The river flowing past Kremmling was named the Grand River by the French, but this designation was changed by Congress in 1921 to its current name of the Colorado River.

Kremmling was incorporated in 1904, and in addition to supporting the area's agricultural community, it was a stage terminal for passengers arriving from the east by train and continuing west via the stage lines.

Located near the confluence of the Blue and Colorado Rivers, this community of 2,000 rests in a valley setting at 7,364 feet.

Agriculture and outdoor recreation head the list of activities here. Tennis, fishing, horseback riding, and camping are available in the immediate area of town, with other recreational activities available in other areas of the valley. Bicycle trails and scenic drives are nearby.

Weekend activities throughout the summer include rodeos, barbeques, roping contests, western dancing, and horse shows.

For the hiking enthusiast, the Gore-Eagle's Nest Wilderness Area is only twenty miles away. For the rockhound, the outcroppings, fossils, and petrified wood in the Wolford Mountain area will be of interest.

Kremmling Memorial Hospital: 724-3442.

Kremmling Ranger Station: 724-3244.

Sheriff: 724-3888.

Kremmling

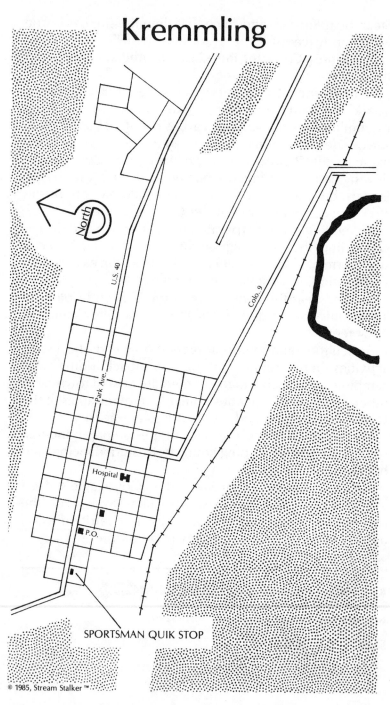

Kremmling

ELKTROUT

A PRIVATE HUNTING AND ANGLING LODGE
ON THE COLORADO RIVER

STEVE HERTER
BOX 614 • KREMMLING, COLO. • 80459
303-724-3343

CONEJOS RIVER

Map Reference 14

This is a beautiful stream located in a beautiful valley about as far south as one can be in Colorado. At its closest, the river flows only three miles from the New Mexico border. The Spanish influence is strongly felt in this part of the state, and most physical entities, whether natural or manmade, carry names in the melodic Spanish language.

The Conejos (meaning "rabbits" in Spanish) River flows for approximately seventy-five miles from its heading in the area of Platoro to its confluence with the Rio Grande River southeast of Alamosa. The river averages fifty to sixty feet in width, offering the angler a wide variety of water types to fish. This is a riffle/pool type river as it drops through the upper valley lined with aspen groves, fir, Englemann spruce, willows, and pinon pine. The riverbanks in many places are thick with willows. The endangered peregrine falcon and bald eagle may sometimes be sighted in the river corridor. In its lower reaches, the river flows more calmly through cottonwood flats, and in this portion of the river, in addition to brown trout, anglers will occasionally hook northern pike that have moved up from the Rio Grande. For these fish, the favorite fare is lures and large streamer flies. An occasional rattlesnake has been reported in this area, so exercise proper caution. Information on this part of the Rio Grande National Forest is available at the Forest Service office, located fourteen miles north of Antonito outside the town of La Jara on Highway 285.

The Conejos is not a river that anglers float. Being rather small in size, it is best waded, and because of deep holes and a relatively deep channel, we recommend chest waders for ease of accessibility to the wide variety of water and to help in crossing.

Private property surrounds the river, but access may sometimes be obtained by asking permission. For the most part, however, this river offers a very high percentage of accessibility, and signs have been posted and stiles built over fences to accommodate considerate anglers. Efforts between the land owners, the Forest Service, and the Division of Wildlife have opened the river for the enjoyment of all of us, and their efforts should be applauded.

Through the four miles immediately below Platoro Reservoir, the river is braided with grassy cutbanks. Fishing is usually good here, particularly early in the season. Above the intersection of the Platoro Reservoir Road and Colorado 17, the Rainbow Trout Lodge controls about fifteen miles of the river. From this intersection downstream to Mogote is the most popular section of the river, and access is very good.

The most plentiful fish in the river is the brown trout, but a fair number of rainbows will also be caught. The average size is about twelve inches, with a good fish considered to be over sixteen inches. Fortunately, the river contains no whitefish, and in order to protect the Rio Grande cutthroat, a no-kill area has been designated on the Lake Fork of the Conejos from the Rock Lake outlet upstream to the headwaters, including Big Lake.

The river runs clear most of the time. Tackle is available at stores in Antonito as well as along the river. For guide service, it is best to inquire at the Conejos Ranch.

Insects

The insect mix on the Conejos is dominated by the caddis fly. Second in quantity are the Mayflies, and there is also a population of small golden stoneflies. The latter come off from mid to late June when the river can be high from runoff, but the clarity of the water makes it worth fishing as a dry fly.

Tackle

For the flyfisherman, a four or five weight outfit is perfectly suited to the size of this river.

Flies and Lures

Dries—Elk Hair Caddis, Adams with an olive body, in addition to standard pattern, Blue Winged Olive, Grey Hackle Peacock, Hendrickson, Red Quill, Mahogony Dun, Humpy, Royal Wulff, all in sizes 14 and 16.

Nymphs—Latex Caddis, Hare's Ear, Renegade, Muskrat, Olive Caddis Larvae in sizes 14 and 16, plus a Golden Stone Nymph in 12.

Streamers—Try a yellow bodied, black winged Matuka or dark Zonkers in large sizes, 2/0 to 2. Lures in the lower river include No. 2 Rooster Tail, Mepps, and Panther Martins.

Osier Creek and Cascade Creek

You can get to both of these wild trout creeks via good gravel roads, well marked from about 12.0 miles west of Antonito south along Bighorn Creek to Osier Park. Osier is a very fragile habitat, the access to the water is difficult, and the fish are small. This is not recommended for serious fishing.

Platoro Reservoir

This lake is located at the headwaters of the Conejos River and offers fishing on 800 acres of very cold and very deep water. Boats are available for rent, and the fishing is for browns and rainbows. Above the reservoir, a trail leads to the "Three Forks"—the North and Middle forks of the Conejos, and El Rito Azul. A trail also leads from the reservoir along the Adams Fork, an inlet stream to the reservoir.

ANTONITO

The community of Antonito is probably best known

81

today as the Colorado starting point for rides on the Cumbres and Toltec Scenic Railroad. Spiked down in 1880, this narrow gauge railroad was built to serve the mining camps of the San Juan Mountains. The term "narrow gauge" was used due to the reduced span (thirty-six inches) between the rails when compared to conventional rails (fifty-six and one-half inches). These narrower tracks, combined with their lighter weight (only sixty-five pounds per yard), allowed track construction to bend around sharper curves and permitted less complex trestles to be built because less weight was involved per loaded car. The narrow gauge lines were eventually doomed, however, because all freight had to be transferred when the narrow gauge met the standard gauge rails. Currently, a one-way/one-day or two-day round-trip scenic ride between Antonito and Chama, New Mexico, takes place daily during summer and fall. The route crosses the state border eleven times, climbs 10,015-foot Cumbres Pass, and stops for a view of spectacular Toltec Gorge, where the Los Pinos River flows 1,000 feet below.

In nearby Conejos is Colorado's oldest church.

Because of the Indians, the New Mexican settlers did not establish themselves in the area until the 1850s. From 1850 to 1880, treaties provided for the removal of the Ute Indians to reservations in western Colorado and Utah. During the 1870s and 1880s, the population of the valley grew substantially as Mormon settlers established communities at Richfield, Ephraim, Sanford, and Manassa. The latter two became prosperous through the growing of wheat, oats, barley, alfalfa, and peas. Manassa is also the birthplace of world-champion boxer Jack Dempsey.

The settlement of Platoro ("plata" in Spanish means silver, and "oro" means gold) was prospected in the 1870s and continued essentially through the turn of the century as a mining center. As such, it declined due to the expense of transporting the ore out of the mine fields. This was to be the fate of many mining areas that were not served by the railroads. Platoro is located forty-five miles northwest of Antonito and serves now as a summer community and recreation center with tourist accommodations. Platoro Reservoir dam backs up the Conejos River for seven and one-half miles, forming the 990-acre impoundment that is the highest manmade lake in North America.

The Conejos district ranger office is located in the town of La Jara. Within this district lie a variety of Indian campsites and artifacts, including stone chips and arrowheads. The entire area was inhabited by the Ute Indians and was considered good hunting ground.

For hikers and horseback riders, consider Three Forks Park, which is the site of the confluence of the Middle Fork of the Conejos River, the North Fork, and El Rito Azul. Trails follow these three creeks, offering good access.

Camping

Camping is available to the west of Antonito along the Conejos River. Five campgrounds are situated between town and Platoro Reservoir, with another at the reservoir. This entire valley is very popular with anglers, and the campgrounds fill early in the day. Between Antonito and the turnoff to Platoro, look for Mogote and Aspen Glade campgrounds. At the turnoff is located Elk Creek Campground. Upstream toward Platoro are Spectacle Lake and Conejos campgrounds. Continuing on Highway 17 over La Manga Pass toward Chama, New Mexico, follow the gravel road north at Cumbres Pass to the Trujillo Meadows Campground.

Numerous commercial camping facilities are located on Highway 17, which follows the lower Conejos River, and on Forest Road 250 following the upper Conejos. Both areas provide lodging, gas, groceries, etc.

Cumbres & Toltec Railroad, P.O. Box 668, Antonito 81120. Phone: 376-5483.

Guadalupe Clinic: 376-5426.

Antonito

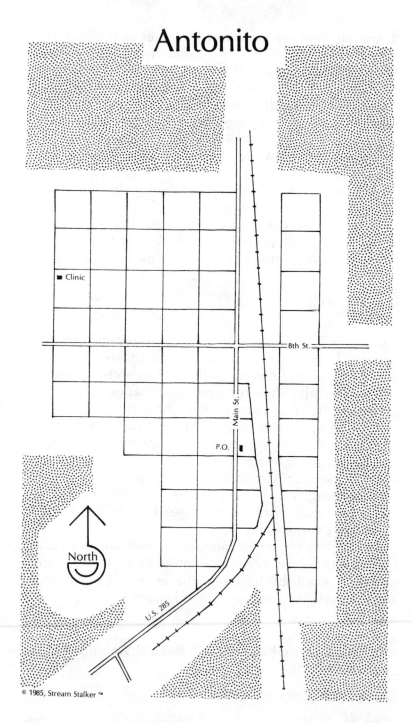

Clinic

8th St.

Main St.

P.O.

North

U.S. 285

© 1985, Stream Stalker ™

EAST RIVER

Map Reference 2

This delightful stream headwaters at Emerald Lake and flows briskly for thirty-five miles from above the old town of Gothic down to the settlement of Almont, where it blends with the water of the Taylor River to form the famous Gunnison River. As it glides across this wide valley, cottonwoods pinch at the fifty-foot width of its boulder-free channel.

Recent changes have reduced the length of river open to the public, so the limited access is now adjacent to the Roaring Judy Hatchery for a short distance above and below the bridge. Private property in both directions will be evident by property line fences and/or no trespassing signs.

The feeling of many local fishermen is that the size and number of fish keep increasing in the restricted water below the hatchery. The opportunity exists throughout the river to catch rainbow, browns, brooks, and the Snake River cutthroat. The predominant insects in the river are caddis, with Brachycentrus hatching April through September and Hydropsyche coming off in September into early October. As for mayflies, the Ephemerella grandis emerges from late June to mid-July, while Ephemerella doddsi rises in August. The emergers and adult imitations of these two large insects work well, especially above the hatchery bridge.

Tackle

Long casts are not required on the East, and therefore a five weight fly outfit is perfect. The fishing here is primarily with wets and dries in medium sizes, and the river is shallow enough that you do not have to use a lot of weight on the leader to sink the wet flies. Hip boots could be used when the water is down, but we would suggest chest waders to allow better mobility.

Flies and Lures

Dries—Elk Hair Caddis in tan and olive are good in sizes 14 and 16. Also, Adams, Grey Wulff, and Humpies. Big Blue Winged Olives are great when imitating the grandis and doddsi hatches. Also try Orange Ashers, Royal Wulff, and Grey Hackle Peacock.

Wets—Muskrat, Hare's Ear, Renegade, and Brown Hackle Peacock, all in Nos. 12 through 16.

CRESTED BUTTE

In 1974, Crested Butte was designated a National Historic District. Situated at approximately 9,000 feet, this is a small town with a big attraction. The false front buildings on Elk Avenue amplify the feeling that you are truly in a restored Victorian community. The spectacular scenery of rugged mountain terrain combines with the subtle sophistication of fine cuisine, cultural activities, and sports opportunities to make this a real family-oriented vacation destination. The residents are proud of their city and do their best to make you welcome.

The gold and silver booms of the 1880s gradually pushed the Ute Indians out of the Crested Butte area as the population and the railroad moved in. The town served as a supply center for the outlying mining camps until the mid-1890s. Its own beginning was as a gold mining camp, but the town is probably best known for its activity in coal mining, which also started in the 1880s. These mines were closed in 1952.

A short drive south from town puts you on the East River. A very short drive in the opposite direction puts you in the town of Mt. Crested Butte, the recently created village at the base of the ski mountain. Here you will find a variety of lodging, shopping, and dining.

Although well known as a ski resort in winter, the summer activities throughout the Crested Butte area include tennis, golf, hiking, theatre, art shows, bike races, music, horseback riding, interesting shopping, and wonderful dining. You will also find a golf school, an annual arts fair, and an aerial weekend. The town has two athletic clubs, a public bath house and spa, buggy rides, and free shuttle buses during the summer.

To the interest of nearly every tourist, the local hardware store has displayed on the wall the world record elk rack which was shot in 1899 about twelve miles west of town.

Camping

Campgrounds are located nearby on the small streams of Coal Creek, Upper East River, Cement Creek, and Ohio Creek.

Chamber of Commerce, 405 Second Avenue. Crested Butte 81224. Phone: 349-6438.

Emergency: 911

Mt. Crested Butte Medical Center: 349-2044.

Crested Butte

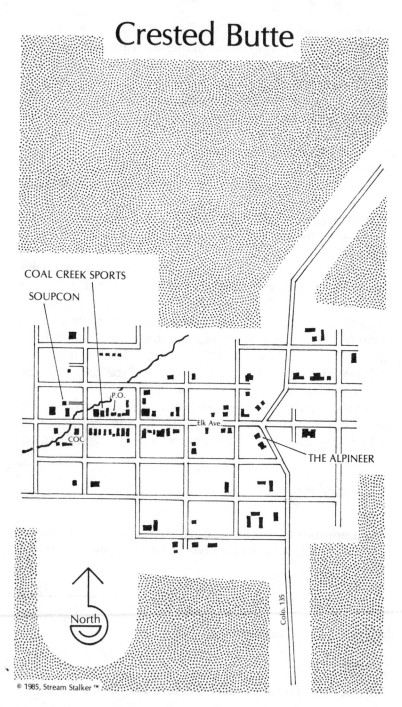

COAL CREEK SPORTS

SOUPCON

P.O.

COC

Elk Ave.

THE ALPINEER

Colo. 135

North

© 1985, Stream Stalker ™

Mt. Crested Butte

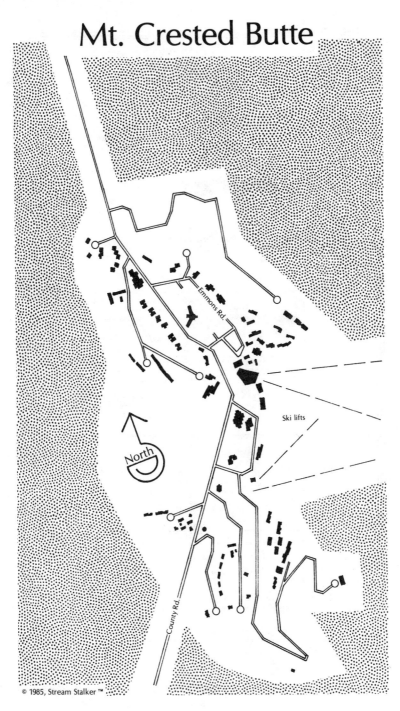

© 1985, Stream Stalker ™

Crested Butte

EAGLE RIVER

Map Reference 15

Although the Eagle River has no official rating as either a Gold Medal or Wild Trout river, we describe it here because of its viability as a trout stream and because one of its tributaries, Gore Creek, is listed among the state's Gold Medal waters.

The Eagle River was named by the Ute Indians who claimed the river had as many tributaries as there are feathers in an eagle's tail. It runs a distance of approximately seventy miles from its headwaters near Tennessee Pass, where it flows northwesterly until it reaches the town of Minturn. Here it turns west and flows approximately thirty-five miles to its confluence with the Colorado River. Through this distance below Minturn, it cuts through a varied landscape of gray and brown sandstone, shale, and gypsum. The gypsum in this valley formed when the seas of this area dried up 280 million years ago. Although not visible from the highway, Colorado's youngest volcano, 4,000 years old, is located just north of Dotsero. The bumpiness you experience in small sections of the highway here is caused by shifting shale layers beneath the roadbed, as the geology of the valley continues on its timeless journey of evolutionary change.

The riparian environment includes a variety of flora with pine, box elder, willows, and cottonwood trees most prevalent. In places, vines can be found growing mountain gooseberries and blueberries.

From the point of view of access, the river can be broken down into segments between the communities that border it. Starting in the upper reaches at the resort of Vail, fishing is available right through town on Gore Creek. Just south of I-70, two miles downstream of the town of Minturn, Gore Creek joins the Eagle. Flowing to Avon and then to Edwards, the river takes on a braided character. This pattern took place when the sediments from the great glaciers of the Sawatch and Gore ranges spread over the Eagle Valley. There is a mile of state property just below the Gore/Eagle confluence, and from this point, the fourteen miles to Wolcott offer a good deal of accessible water intermixed with private areas where permission is required. Any access here is gained from U.S. Highway 6.

Between Wolcott and Eagle, the access is very good, with much of the river available because of a state lease extending for about six miles on the north side of the river. Watch for posted property here, as some land is totally private, and some is open with permission. Entrance to the water from Eagle down to Gypsum is difficult because the river flows through private property here, and permission would have to be obtained from the land owners.

Below Gypsum, the land is mostly controlled by the Bureau of Land Management and is open to fishing. This six miles of river to Dotsero runs slowly through the cottonwood flats, and the riverbed is heavily silted. The water here is rather deep and not well suited to wading. Access is good, with several lanes leading to the river from the main road. The banks are thick with willows, so casting a fly can be tricky. There is a picnic site 4.3 miles upstream from Dotsero. Floating through this area is probably the most effective way to fish it because of the water depth and riparian foliage.

Generally speaking, the river offers about forty miles of varied type water, about sixty feet in width, with clear water appearing after the runoff near the end of June barring excessive rain. This river does cloud easily after rainstorms due to the turbidity caused by both Brush Creek and Milk Creek as they enter the Eagle after flowing out of their gypsum cliffs. The best time to fish the Eagle is from July through October. Local information on conditions can be obtained either in Eagle or Glenwood Springs, and guided fishing is available out of Glenwood.

The fish population ratios vary with location in the river, with estimates as follows: Upper River, about 80 percent browns to 20 percent rainbows; Near Eagle, about 50/50; Lower River, about 30 percent browns to 70 percent rainbows. The fish in the upper river will average about twelve inches, while the lower river fish will average closer to thirteen inches.

This is essentially a caddis fly river, with their population estimated at about 80 percent of the total, with stoneflies and mayflies comprising the balance.

Tackle

Five and six weight fly rods are adequate with floating lines. For spinning, four pound lines are common. We would recommend chest waders with felt soles to maneuver over the cobble bottom that can be very slippery, particularly later in the season. Cleats would be helpful if you have them.

Flies and Lures

Dries—Adams, Elk Hair Caddis, Goddard Caddis, Letort Hopper, and Humpy in 14 and 16.

Nymphs—Olive bodied patterns work well, both in caddis and stonefly imitations.

Traditional wet flies include the Renegade and Brown Hackle Peacock in sizes 8 to 12, and a Prince Nymph in No. 12. In June, try a big No. 4 dark brown stone nymph.

Streamers—Platte River Special, Matuka, and Muddlers

are good patterns.

Terrestrials—Red and Black Ants are good in size 18, and hoppers are a good bet in August.

Lures—Panther Martin, Mepps, Kastmaster, and Super Vibrax.

VAIL

The Vail Valley is located 100 miles west of Denver. It is, of course, known internationally as one of Colorado's finest ski areas. Situated on Highway I-70 at 8,200 feet, it is considered America's largest resort. In addition to fishing possibilities, Vail offers a wide variety of summer and fall activities. There are five eighteen-hole golf courses, over seventy tennis courts, many swimming pools, horseback riding, hiking, ice skating, bike trails, and rides up the mountainsides on gondolas and chairlifts.

Prior to 1939, Vail was another wild piece of Colorado countryside. During that year, under the engineering supervision of Charlie Vail, Highway 6 was constructed out of Denver to points west through this valley. Four members of the army's World War II Tenth Mountain Division envisioned the area's potential as a ski resort, and with investors from Denver started planning its future. Vail Mountain opened to its first skiers back in 1962.

Many events occur throughout the summer, including golf and tennis tournaments, bike races, music festivals, rodeos, and theatre.

Camping

One-half mile east of East Vail is located the Gore Creek

Campground with seventeen campsites with water and toilets. This area offers access to the trailhead to the Eaglenest Wilderness. The site is reached off old U.S. Highway 6, just south of Gore Creek.

Vail Resort Association: 476-1000.
241 East Meadow Drive
Vail, CO 81657

Vail Valley Medical center: 476-2451.

Vail Police: 476-7000.

Vail

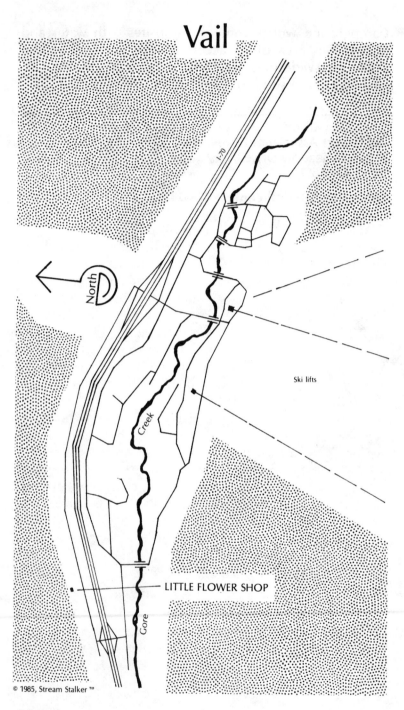

I-70

North

Creek

Ski lifts

Gore

LITTLE FLOWER SHOP

© 1985, Stream Stalker ™

EAGLE

The community of Eagle is situated on the river of the same name approximately midway between Glenwood Springs and the well-known ski resort of Vail. Prior to gaining its permanent name of Eagle in 1896, the town had been called several names, including Castle, Brush, Eagle River Crossing, and McDonald.

With the white man progressing westward into the Colorado gold and silver camps, the Ute Indians were finally displaced from the valley and relocated to eastern Utah in the 1870s. Cattle were brought to the valley in 1880. Gold and silver were discovered at a nearby area called Fulford, and the village of Eagle became a stage stop and outfitting center for the mining camp.

Although Eagle is still an agricultural support community, it is becoming increasingly more tourist-oriented, as ski resorts continue to cover the landscape of the upper Eagle River Valley.

Using Eagle as a base, the visitor has access to many activities in the valley. Several eighteen-hole golf courses are located upstream toward Vail, as are tennis courts, hiking, and swimming. Several auto tours can originate from Eagle for both passenger car and four-wheel drive vehicles. Rafting companies are available in the valley and offer trips down the nearby Colorado River.

Camping

Opportunities for camping are plentiful in the Eagle vicinity. Several campgrounds lie northeast of Eagle along the Coffee Pot Springs Road. Directions are as follows: Travel fourteen miles west of Eagle on I-70 to the Dotsero exit, number 133, then follow the signs for Sweetwater and

Burns, turning north on the Colorado River Road. Follow this road for 1.8 miles, then turn left onto Forest Road 600—the Coffee Pot Springs Road. Travel 16.7 miles on Road 600 to Coffee Pot Springs Campground. Fifteen sites are available in an aspen grove. Trailers are welcome. Water and picnic tables are available. The elevation here is 10,100 feet.

Following this same road, at mile 26.9 is the turnoff to White Owl Lake Campground (one mile off of Road 600). Passenger cars and trailers under twenty-two feet are okay. There are five sites here with toilets but no drinking water. The lake is twenty acres in size, with fishing for rainbow and brook trout. The lake is shallow, with an eleven- to twenty-four-foot depth.

At mile 27.7, turn onto Forest Road 640. Kline's Folly campsite is on the left with four units. The road to Heart Lake intersects on the right about one-half mile further down Road 640, and a short distance further on the left is Supply Basin Campground with six units. These areas have toilets, but no drinking water. The shallow shoreline at Heart Lake makes bank fishing difficult.

Deep Lake Campground is at mile 29 on Road 600. Located at 10,500 feet, the area has twenty-five campsites, toilets, but no drinking water. No motorboats are allowed on this thirty-seven-acre lake. This is a very popular area and is one place where President Teddy Roosevelt camped with a hunting party in 1905. The Colorado record lake trout of thirty-six pounds was caught here.

Another camping area nearby is at Sweetwater Lake. After turning onto the Colorado River Road at exit 133 at Dotsero, continue north for seven miles, then turn left onto the Sweetwater road and travel for another nine miles. At the lake, turn left across Sweetwater Creek and follow the road into the campground, where there are nine sites. Water is sporadically available from a spring; toilets are available, and trailers under twenty-two feet are permitted. Boats can be rented at the private resort on the north shore, and a dock is located at the campground. The elevation here is 7,700 feet.

To the south of Eagle, follow Brush Creek Road 400 for 10.1 miles, then turn left on Road 415 and go 5.7 and 6 miles to Yeoman Park and Fulford Cave campgrounds, respectively. Between the two there are twenty-four campsites, toilets, and drinking water; trailers are discouraged.

If you travel sixteen miles south of Eagle on Road 400, you will come to Sylvan Lake Campground. This is a very popular area with fifty campsites. Boating and fishing on forty-five-acre Sylvan Lake are available. Trailers are allowed, and toilets and drinking water are present.

Emergency: 911.

Eagle Medical Clinic: 328-6357.

Town of Eagle, 108 W. 2nd Street, Eagle. Phone: 328-6354.

U.S. Forest Service, 125 W. 5th Street, Eagle. Phone: 328-6388.

Eagle

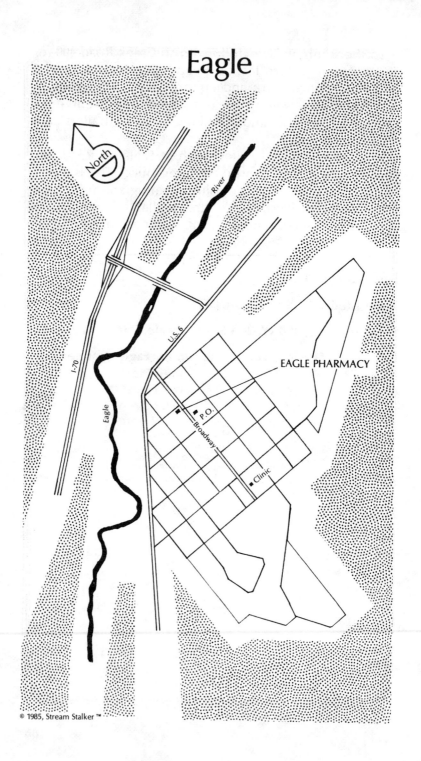

Vail

𝒫sst...
...send flowers home

CALL
THE LITTLE FLOWER SHOP
Vail — 476-3115
Dillon — 468-5498
Breckenridge — 453-1323
Major Credit Cards Accepted

Eagle

River Notes

GUNNISON RIVER

Map Reference 16 & 17

From its beginning at the community of Almont, the Gunnison flows approximately seventy-five miles to the confluence with its North Fork near Austin. Because this portion of the river is of most interest to anglers, we describe it in some detail. The East River from the north and the Taylor River from the east join and mix at Almont, forming the point of origin of the once great Gunnison. Its former reputation as one of this country's great trout rivers must remain on the pages of history and on the minds and photographs of those anglers who had the good fortune to fish the river at its prime. It still remains a fine stream, but unfortunately its bounty has been severely diminished.

Its first twenty miles pass mostly through private property. The water open to public fishing includes about three miles directly below Almont to the forest boundary. From this point to the Neversink Picnic Area located five miles below the town of Gunnison, the river flows through private land. From Neversink to the inlet to Blue Mesa Reservoir, there are about five miles of fishing when the reservoir is low and about one-half mile when the reservoir is full.

Throughout its length, the river averages 80 to 100 feet in width and flows with volumes necessitating chest waders. The bottom can become very slick, particularly in the lower reaches near Neversink, and felt soles should be worn. The river flows steadily through willow and cottonwood flats, passing ranches, lodges, and private residences along the way. Due to erosion caused by high water volumes during runoff in recent years, the river channel contains a large number of downed cottonwood trees in the Neversink area, giving excellent cover to fish holding in deep holes next to the bank.

As the largest instate tributary to the Colorado River, the Gunnison is also the largest river in Colorado, whose entire basin lies within the borders of the state. Another dubious distinction unique to the river is the fact that it houses more large reservoirs than any other river complex in the state.

Tackle

The size and character of this river suggest the use of five and six weight fly rod systems with floating lines adequate for all but possibly streamer fishing in the fall. A sink-tip would work well in the lower reaches for this purpose. Spin fishermen will want to use four-pound test lines.

Flies and Lures

Standard patterns work very well on the Gunnison. For dries, try Adams, Elk Hair and Goddard Caddis, Irresistible, Humpy, Rio Grande King, and Orange Asher in sizes 12 to 16. Caddis patterns work especially well early in the season. Wet flies include Hare's Ear Nymph, Renegade, Western Coachman, Rio Grande King, Woolly Worms, caddis larvae, and stonefly nymphs. Most work well in Nos. 12 to 16, with the Woolly Worms and stone nymphs best in 4 to 8. Streamers such as Muddler Minnows, Marabou Muddlers, Woolly Buggers, and Zonkers are favorites, particularly in the fall. Lures such as Mepps, Panther Martins, and Rapalas will do the job.

Curecanti National Recreation Area

This area in the path of the Gunnison River is composed of three reservoirs. From east to west, upstream to downstream, they are Blue Mesa, Morrow Point, and Crystal. Almost all of the recreation involved here centers around Blue Mesa. With a shoreline of ninety-six miles, this is the largest and longest reservoir in Colorado. Its surface is enjoyed by boaters, fishermen, and water skiers, with boats for rent at the Elk Creek Marina. The visitor center at Elk Creek conducts programs to familiarize visitors with the activities available throughout the area. The subsurface canyons and channels of Blue Mesa provide refuge to lake trout, browns, rainbows, brooks, and kokanee salmon.

The Morrow Point and Crystal reservoirs lie deep in canyons carved through Precambrian rock by the Gunnison River. Access to these impoundments is difficult, and any watercraft used must be hand carried to the water via hiking trails. Local regulations, conditions, and directions should be obtained from official sources within the area.

The name of this recreation area comes from Chief Curicata of the Utes, who at one time hunted the Colorado territory.

The most successful fishing is done with large streamer flies casting out from shore, or from a boat casting in toward shore. The inlets on Blue Mesa are the most productive areas to fish.

Lower Gunnison River

Within the Black Canyon National Monument itself there are two hiking trails popular with fishermen. Grizzly Gulch Trail goes to the river from the north rim, and Warner Point Trail from the south rim. Total time on these trails for the round trip, top to bottom to top, is usually between six and eight hours, so plans must be made in advance to allow enough time to make the trip during daylight hours. Obtain detailed directions on these trails at monument headquarters.

The Gunnison River below the monument offers an air of adventure to a degree not found on the other rivers in this book. This section of river is in the Gunnison Gorge, and to fish the better sections requires that the angler either float with a commercial guide service, hike down steep walls into the canyon from above, or walk up the riverbank from downstream. This is *not* a "drive to" section of the Gunnison. The options in more detail are as follows:

1. Guide service is available out of the towns of Hotchkiss and Montrose.

2. Hiking into the gorge is done from trailheads on the plateau above from the west side of the river as it flows from the monument north toward the community of Austin. The main artery is a gravel road to the south from Austin which terminates at Olathe. This is called the Peach Valley Road, and to find it, local inquiry may be required. From it, side roads take off toward the river. Each road should be marked with a Bureau of Land Management

sign. The roads are not maintained and can be considered more like trails than actual roads. Vehicles without high clearance should not be driven in this area. Four-wheel drive vehicles are best suited, but under rainy conditions, even they can falter on the adobe-type earth which, when wet, becomes extremely slippery and next-to-impossible to drive. There are three of these roads, and they all terminate at trailheads beyond which foot traffic is required to get down to the river. All gear is hand carried from this point.

The first road is the Ute Trail. It turns off Peach Valley Road five miles from Austin. It is then two and one-half miles to the trailhead, and a four-and-one-half-mile hike to the river. Once at the river, you can fish both up and downstream for a total of about four miles. The river here is in an open valley and can be waded.

The second road is called the Duncan Trail, and it joins the Peach Valley Road about nine and one-half miles from Austin. A drive of about two miles will put you at the trailhead of a very steep, three-fourths-mile hike to the river straight down the canyon side on loose rocks. The river at this point is not conducive to wading, so fishing is done from the bank in very deep pools and runs.

The third entrance from the Peach Valley Road is the Chukkar Trail, located thirteen and one-half miles from Austin. The drive here totals 7.7 miles to the trailhead, with a one-mile hike to the river, covering a descent of approximately one thousand vertical feet. This is about a forty-five-minute hike down, and an hour and a half return trip. This hike is not recommended for people in poor physical condition or having any heart or pulmonary problems. When you reach the river, there is no wading, but you can bank fish for one-fourth mile downstream and two miles upstream.

On any of these hike-in trips, be sure to take drinking water, or be prepared to purify the river water. Also, take proper gear for protection against rainstorms. Be confident that you are physically able to make these strenuous hikes so you do not have to be the subject of a rescue party. Never travel alone on an expedition of this nature. Take a friend or two!

The water in the area of both the Chukkar and Duncan trails is really best fished from a boat with a professional guide. On occasion, individuals will carry boats into the river at the Ute Trail and float down to the Forks. Anyone thinking of doing this on his own should be advised that there is difficult water throughout this section, with four major rapids rated to Class IV. A knowledge of the river is needed here, and these rapids should be scouted ahead of time if the boater is new to the area.

3. The last option of walking upstream would start at the Forks—the confluence of the North Fork with the Gunnison River itself. The starting point is reached by driving eight miles west of Hotchkiss on Highway 92. A turn to the left at the BLM sign stating "Gunnison Forks—River Access" will take you to the confluence one mile away. At this point, walk about 300 yards upstream of the confluence along the North Fork, where you ford the river to be in a position to fish the main Gunnison from the east bank. You can walk and fish upstream to the Smith Fork, which is a distance of about 3.8 miles.

The upper reaches of the gorge contain very deep pools, and one should be careful not to step off a bank into swift water, as some of the holes in this area are estimated to be twenty to thirty feet deep. Due to electrical power demands downstream, the flows in this section of the Gunnison can fluctuate considerably, and the angler should keep this in mind when wading. The flows can vary as much as 1,000 cfs while you are at the river, but fishing is at its best when the flow is between 800 and 1,200 cfs. Water information can be obtained from the Uncompahgre River Water Users Association in Montrose at (303) 249-3813. If you camp in the gorge, be sure to put your gear above the highwater line to assure its safety.

At the confluence of the North Fork, the predominant fish is the rainbow, and remains so up the river for six to seven miles, when the ratio starts to change and browns become predominant throughout the upper reaches of the gorge. The average size of the fish throughout this entire section of river is about thirteen inches. The biggest fish are taken on wet flies in the deep holes, but will also be taken in close, right off the cutbanks.

The fisherman should enjoy not only the fishing on this section of the river, but should also take time out to appreciate his surroundings as well. This is a rather remote area by most angling standards on well-known rivers, and here one has the opportunity to sight resident golden eagles, transient bald eagles, the nationally endangered peregrine falcon, and river otter, bighorn sheep, elk, deer, black bear, and grasshoppers in the Johnson grass. In fall, the turning leaves on the willows, box elder, and scrub oak of the lower water stand in stark contrast to the dark canyon walls of the upper gorge.

Tackle

This stretch of river puts greater stress on tackle than most water in Colorado because of the depth of the holes and the type of terminal tackle needed for best results. The bigger fish are caught on weighted nymphs fished on larger than normal tippet diameters, with leaders carrying an abundant number of lead weights, with said leader possibly attached to a lead-core fly line. In total, this arrangement becomes a formidable challenge to cast, so our recommendation on fly tackle is to use lines of seven or eight weight, with nine-foot rods to match. You will also appreciate the power of these rods when playing larger fish in the heavy current typical of the river in this canyon.

The insects here are primarily caddis flies, with stoneflies running second and mayflies third. The large Pteronarcys californica, or willow fly as it is referred to locally, is especially effective near the Forks in July when fished as a larval imitation. Other favorite wet flies include the Hare's Ear in sizes 10 to 14, and the Bitch Creek, Girdle Bug,

Woolly Bugger, Woolly Worms, and Muddler Minnows in sizes 4 to 8. Dry fly favorites are Rio Grande King, Royal Wulff, Orange Asher, and Adams in sizes 12 to 16. Also favored is a Black Gnat in sizes 18 and 20, along with other midge imitations. The favorite lure here is the Panther Martin. Best colors are a gold blade with a yellow body, or a yellow body with black spots.

Lake Fork of the Gunnison

Highway 149 heads south from Highway 50 at the eastern end of Blue Mesa Reservoir. Following 149 for 24.6 miles will bring you to Gateview, where you turn right (north) at a sign stating, "Red Bridge 2 mi., Gateview Campground 7 mi." From this turnoff, it is 2.4 miles to the red bridge, which is actually red. This stretch of the Lake Fork flows through private property, but immediately prior to arriving at the bridge, you will find a small state recreation area for picnicking. From this point downstream, a gravel road parallels the river for about five miles as the stream tumbles through a canyon covered with pine and scrub oak. The road deadends here at Gateview Campground, but the river continues a few more miles until it empties into Blue Mesa Reservoir. This entire section, from the bridge to the reservoir, is open to fishing. No trailers are allowed beyond the bridge.

The river through this canyon is about thirty feet wide, offering a variety of water types. After runoff when the river returns to its normal level, fishing can be done in hip boots. The river fishes well with both nymphs and dries, the latter particularly effective in the evenings. As a feeder stream to a large reservoir, the Lake Fork can be particularly attractive to late season anglers who like to fish over brown trout as they move into the stream in search of spawning gravel.

Use standard fly dressings in sizes 14 to 18 to imitate the caddis and Mayflies of this stream. In the fall, of course, fish streamers such as Zonkers, Matukas, and Spruce Flies.

The river above Gateview is almost entirely on private property. There are a few short sections of water next to the road, but for the most part it is closed to fishing.

GUNNISON

This community on the Gunnison River was named for Captain John W. Gunnison, who explored this region for the U.S. government in 1853 seeking a transcontinental railroad route through Colorado and into Utah. In the late 1870s, gold and silver were found in all directions from Gunnison, and the site became a shipping and supply center.

Gunnison County covers an area larger than Connecticut and has only 13,000 permanent residents. The city of Gunnison is situated at an elevation of 7,703 feet with a population of approximately 6,000. The citizens are well accustomed to hosting tourists, since an estimated one million visitors pass through the valley every year.

Summer activities center around fishing, bike racing, golf tournaments, rodeos, and art festivals.

One of the most famous personalities of the Gunnison country was Alferd (not Alfred) Packer, who was nicknamed "The Colorado Cannibal" after killing and eating his companions when stranded near Lake City in a ferocious winter storm in 1874. The area north of Lake City, southwest of Gunnison, is known as Cannibal Plateau.

An interesting side trip from Gunnison would include the forty-one-mile drive to Alpine Tunnel, constructed in 1880 by the Denver, South Park and Pacific Railroad. It continued in use until 1910. This abandoned railroad tunnel is 1,771 feet long and punctures through the continental divide at 11,620 feet. In its day, it was the highest railroad tunnel in the world. You will be able to see the collapsed tunnel entrance, the stone engine house, a small depot, and the engine turntable. You can walk between the west and east portals of the tunnel over 11,940-foot Altman Pass. Maps of this area are available from the Chamber of Commerce, along with other maps that elaborate auto tours lasting from one hour to all day.

Two places of interest are the towns of Almont and Tincup. Almont is located ten miles north of Gunnison and is a summer tourist community. It was once the busy terminal for a branch of the Denver and South Park Railroad. Ore from many of the mining camps in the area was brought here for rail shipment out. Tincup is a ghost town just southeast of Taylor Park Reservoir to the northeast of Gunnison. In 1882 it boasted a population of 6,000. Today, it is one of the state's most popular ghost towns.

To the west of town is the Black Canyon of the Gunnison National Monument. This area represents the deepest and most spectacular twelve miles of the total gorge. The Black Canyon derives its name from the fact that the gray canyon walls are darkened in shadows most of the day.

The depth of the canyon ranges from 1,730 to 2,700 feet. Its width goes down to forty feet at the river and to 1,300 feet at the rim in an area known as the narrows. Views are excellent on the south rim along a paved eight-mile drive with twelve overlooks, and with a gravel four-mile drive on the north rim with seven overlooks. Camping is available on both rims during the summer months.

The Gunnison area provides accommodations in more than seventy motels. Transportation includes scheduled bus and airline service to Gunnison daily from Denver.

Camping

North of Gunnison, several campgrounds are available for both tent and vehicle camping. Along the Taylor River Road 742, there are seven campgrounds, and two more are located on the road along Spring Creek, accessed from 742 to the north. In Taylor Park above the Taylor Dam to the foot of Taylor Pass, another five campgrounds are available.

Chamber of Commerce, Box 36, Gunnison 81230. Phone: 641-1501.

Emergency: City of Gunnison, 201 W. Virginia. Phone: 641-2448

Gunnison National Forest, 216 No. Colorado. Phone: 641-0471.

Division of Wildlife, 300 W. New York. Phone: 641-0088.

Gunnison

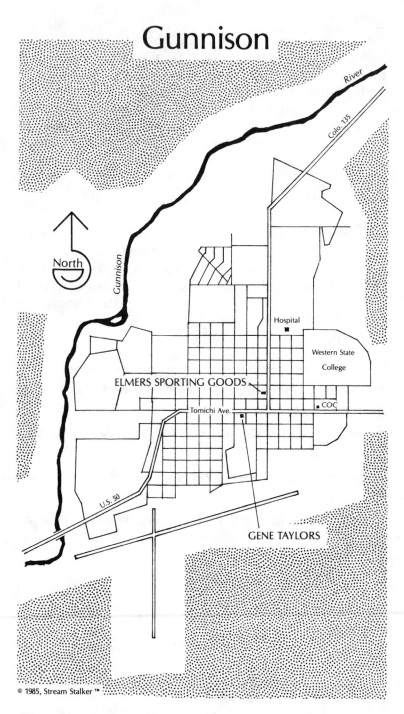

River

Colo. 135

North

Gunnison

Hospital

Western State
College

ELMERS SPORTING GOODS

COC

Tomichi Ave.

U.S. 50

GENE TAYLORS

© 1985, Stream Stalker ™

114

Gunnison

LARAMIE RIVER

Map Reference 5

North from Highway 14 near Chambers Lake, the Laramie River is paralleled by Forest Road 190 for about twenty-seven miles to the Wyoming border. The upper reaches are open to the public for approximately ten miles downstream to the Rawah Dude Ranch. This portion of the river meanders through hay meadows, where the river is fringed with thick willows. The entire river also has a thick population of mosquitoes, so be sure to take your repellent! The river is private below the ranch until you reach the Hohnholz State Wildlife Area near the road bridge going across the river toward the Hohnholz Lakes. This bridge is about six miles from the Wyoming line. This lease extends in both directions from the bridge for a total distance of approximately two and one-half miles. The Hohnholz Ranch is adjacent to the Colorado-Wyoming border and controls access to about four and one-half miles of the river from the border upstream for this entire distance. This area is sometimes open to fishing upon securing permission in advance from the ranch owner.

The river is not difficult to wade, and is usually clear and fishable somewhat earlier than most Colorado rivers, with pleasant fishing for the predominant brown trout throughout June. For small stream/small fish environments, permission may be granted to fish the tributaries of McIntyre Creek and West Creek.

Tackle requirements on the Laramie include insect repellent, a four or five weight fly rod and a selection of standard flies with Elk Hair Caddis, Goddard Caddis, and Adams in sizes 14 to 18 heading the list of favorite dry flies. Tan and green caddis larvae imitations should be fished near the bottom during the day when the fish are not rising.

Chambers Lake

At the headwaters of the Poudre and Laramie rivers, you will find 350-acre Chambers Lake. Although no boats are available to rent at the lake, trolling is popular for rainbows, kokanee salmon, and some lake trout. Occasionally, browns and cutthroat are caught. The lake is approximately two miles long by one-half mile wide and fishes best in October as the aspen leaves turn to gold with the crisp fall weather.

MIDDLE FORK OF THE SOUTH PLATTE

Map Reference 6

The Middle Fork rises west of Hoosier Pass and meanders through the cattle ranches of Middle Park. This is a small, relatively slow stream with plenty of cutbanks as it cuts between willows and pastures. The water is home primarily to brown trout, and a few good-size ones have been known to come out of the cutbanks. But for the most part, the fish average about ten inches. Mosquitoes are a problem here, particularly early in the summer, so don't fish without having some repellent handy.

Most fishing is done by walking the banks as opposed to wading, so hip boots are all that is required. The river fishes best when the water is slightly off-color, but a downpour causing dirty water will put the fish down until it starts to clear. The water here comes up in the spring like most Colorado streams, and the most favorable conditions will occur around the Fourth of July.

Streamer flies work well here, particularly a Zonker, but try some others as well. Dig into the nymph box and try a Hare's Ear or a Woolly Worm—they are favorites when fished close to the bottom.

NORTH PLATTE RIVER

North Park is encircled by the Medicine Bow Mountains to the east, the Never Summers to the northeast, the Rabbit Ears to the South, and the Park Range to the west—all pouring their waters into the North Platte River. The French explorers gave it the name Riviere de Plat, the flat river. This river flows through ranch country, the flat bottomland of North Park—not a mountainside near the continental divide.

Looking at the map of this northern border country of the state you find a marked lack of Indian and Spanish names for the local landmarks—Glendevey, Kings Canyon, Gould, Michigan, Rand, Coalmont. The influence of the white settler is evident in names of both social and geographical locations across the entire northern part of the state. In contrast, it is interesting to run your finger across the map at the bottom of the stae, a mere 250 miles away, and read the names in print. It reveals vividly the variety of rich cultural heritage found in Colorado.

The character of the rivers flowing through North Park must be described as primarily meadow-type water. Relatively slow moving with no dramatic riffles or rapids, the river offers enough riffles and pools to make the fishing interesting and challenging. The streams are bordered with willows in many places, and though not always easy to cast around, the brush-lined banks do provide good holding water for the trout. Wading here is easy when done, but a lot of the fishing is of the crawl and cast type where you are sneaking around on your knees rather than presenting a tall silhouette. When normal volumes of water fill the streams, cutbanks offer inviting targets for your artificial flies, but at times, irrigation draw can pull the flows down to barely a trickle. Usually after July the irrigation demands are minimal and the streams are in normal flow. Due to the large amount of irrigation necessary, you can plan on a formidable mosquito problem through the early part of the summer. Don't forget to have plenty of effective repellent whenever you are on a river or lake in this area.

Walden is the center of economic activity in North Park and provides accommodations, dining, and shopping. From Walden, the fishing is all within a very few miles. From here it is a short drive to the state leases on the North Platte and the Michigan rivers—the two of most interest to the fisherman. The Platte is a slow river with essentially a silted bottom and little cover for the fish. The Michigan is a bit smaller but has more character than the Platte. It is considered the favorite with local anglers. It is about twenty-five feet wide and requires a careful approach so as not to spook the fish. Flyfishing is most productive when pursuing the predominant brown trout population of the river. Browns are estimated to be in numbers as high as 80 percent of the fish present. There are no whitefish in these waters, but rainbows are caught, as well as brook trout in the upper reaches of the streams.

The water is usually fishable the third week of June, with the best hatches taking place the last week of June and into the first two weeks of July. Insects are abundant, with caddis being the most plentiful, Mayflies in good numbers, and stoneflies in quantities enough to turn a trout's head.

Several lease arrangements have been made with the ranchers in North Park, and these leases have made it easier to find water to fish. They are marked, and the property on which you fish should receive the respect it deserves.

Tackle

Due to the size of these streams, lightweight tackle is preferred. Use a fly rod of 4 or 5 weights, and spin lines of two or three pounds. Waders are not needed here. Hip boots are adequate. Tackle is available in Walden. Inquire about guide service.

Flies and Lures

Dries—Adams and Elk Hair Caddis in No. 14 and 16, American March Brown No. 10, Humpy and Royal Wulff, Nos. 14-18.

Nymphs—Muskrat No. 10, Gold Ribbed Hare's Ear and Renegade No. 14, Amber Stonefly in No. 6, Black Woolly Worm No. 8.

Streamers—Zonker and Black Woolly Bugger in Nos. 4 and 6, Mickey Finn in high water.

Local Lakes

There are four lakes near Walden which are of substantial interest to fishermen. The first is Delaney Buttes Lakes. This is a group of three lakes from 67 to 160 acres in size, located nine miles west of town. These lakes are spring fed and sit exposed in sagebrush flats with no protection from the wind. In all three you will find a variety of trout, but each lake is known for a single species: North Lake, browns; South Lake, rainbows; and East Lake, brooks. The cold spring water of these lakes produces great numbers and variety of insect life. Most remembered are prolific hatches of caddis flies in a variety of sizes and colors coming off the water at one time. The fish come to these nervous flies on the surface as well as slightly beneath the surface while the insects are still in the emerging pupal stage. Damsel flies are also very abundant in the lakes, and imitations of the nymphal form slowly worked on the bottom can provide action when all else fails.

These lakes are most productive early and late in the season, and early and late in the day, with a good deal of fishing being done after dark. Camping is available along the lakeshore, and boats with motors are allowed. In addition to trolling spinners and Rapalas behind boats, some anglers prefer to anchor off the shoreline weed beds and cast toward the shore. Weeds become somewhat of a problem later in the summer.

Lake John is another very popular lake in this area. It is also located west of town on well-marked roads. This is a shallow lake with plenty of weed beds and a fair share of large trout. The fishing characteristics here are about the same as on Delaney Buttes. Good populations of damsel and caddis flies keep the flyfisherman busy off the weed beds. This 550-acre lake provides browns, rainbow, and cutthroat trout.

Fly patterns generally good in all the lakes include olive damsel nymphs, No. 12, chartreuse bodies fore and aft fly with brown hackles, Hornberg in late June, fished dry or just under the surface, and caddis larva of bright green body and black head in size No. 12. Fish this one unweighted just below the surface.

All of these lakes are suitable for fishing from a raft or belly-boat, and the method is good because it allows you to get out beyond the weed beds.

One additional body of water in the area for consideration is Cowdrey Lake. This is not as reliable as the other lakes from an angling point of view due to occasional winter kill. It is a small lake of about eighty acres, and does have a good density of scuds and damsel flies. Imitations of these two food forms work well, as does the Hornberg, which is a very popular fly in all the lakes of the area. This is a shallow lake, and the fish are rather small. Because of its size, fishing from a belly-boat is a lot of fun.

WALDEN

The wind has been known to blow across the vast expanse of North Park, and the snow that you see packed against snow fences in winter attests to its regularity. In this park, the small and friendly community of Walden straddles Highway 125, and here the visitor enjoys wonderful views of the majestic peaks of the Routt National Forest to the west and south, and the Colorado State Forest to the east.

The floor of this wide valley is home to cattle ranches, hay meadows, sagebrush, and a large herd of antelope. It is very convenient for the traveler to view fifty or more of these graceful pronghorns grazing nonchalantly but alertly on the opposite side of the fence paralleling the highway. Keep your camera ready and your eyes open, as they do tend to blend into their surroundings under some light conditions.

Camping

East of Walden, bordering the town of Gould, is Colorado State Forest—a mountain setting of 72,000 acres. Activities here include hiking, lake and stream fishing, camping, and four-wheeling. Elevations range from 8,500 to 12,500 feet. It is accessible from Fort Collins, 75 miles away, and from Denver, 150 miles away. There are seventy-five campsites for tents, trailers, and pickup campers. Trailheads exist that lead to five different lakes.

To the west of Walden, available by good roads, lie Lake John and the three Delaney Buttes Lakes. These popular recreation areas serve both anglers and boaters, and offer camping in a totally unwooded environment.

North Park Ranger District, 612 5th St., P.O. Box 158, Walden 80480. Phone: 723-4707.

Colorado State Forest, Star Route, Box 91, Walden. Phone: 723-8366.

Walden

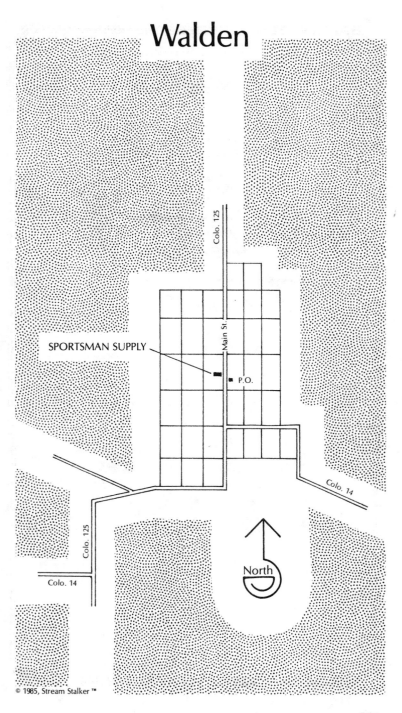

SPORTSMAN SUPPLY

P.O.

Colo. 125

Main St

Colo. 14

Colo. 125

Colo. 14

North

Walden

BIG THOMPSON RIVER

We include the Big Thompson in this guide because it flows through one of the most popular tourist areas in the state, and because of its proximity to the Wild Trout designated North St. Vrain Creek nearby. We feel that many fishermen who might not fish the St. Vrain would like to fish the Big Thompson because of its larger size and easier accessibility.

Within very recent history, and to a degree more vividly than the residents of Estes Park care to remember, the physical character of the Big Thompson has been altered due to the ravages of flashflooding. In both 1976 and 1982, the river became a conduit through which floodwater made its frantic escape from the mountains to the plains. Signs of the devastation remain, but man and nature have repaired the river's wounds to some degree, and the angler can again enjoy relaxing hours on the river.

This stream gathers in Rocky Mountain National Park, flows through Lake Estes, and continues for nineteen miles through the Big Thompson Canyon to emerge from the foothills at the city of Loveland. The fishing area below Estes Park starts at the Lake Estes Dam and continues for approximately thirteen miles to a dam that can virtually dry the riverbed below it. The area for about a mile below the Lake Estes dam is a private ranch with no fishing allowed. Below that section, the access for fishing is very good, with only scattered pieces of private property.

From Estes Park downstream to the end of the canyon, the riverside is dotted with facilities for lodging, dining, and shopping. Traffic through this area is very heavy during the summer with visitors using this road to get to Estes Park and Rocky Mountain National Park.

The river is stocked with rainbows, which is the predominant fish caught, with the average size being about ten inches. The insect in most abundance is the caddis, with mayflies, stoneflies, and midges also important in the trout's diet. The midges are particularly active and vulnerable from March to May.

The river offers a wide variety of water types throughout its length, with plenty of riffles and pockets typical of canyon water. Its thirty-foot width can usually be waded with hip boots, but felt soles are a must as the streambed accumulates moss and becomes very slippery. Although the water will stay high in the spring to accommodate irrigation needs downstream, it will run clear and be fishable because the water is retained in Lake Estes prior to release into the lower river channel.

Tackle

Fly anglers need only a four to five weight outfit here, and spin fishermen can get by with two to four pound line. Chest waders will allow more mobility when the river is at higher levels, but hip boots will suffice a good deal of the time. Equipment and guide service are available in Estes Park.

Flies and Lures

Popular dry flies include the Humpy, Adams, Elk Hair Caddis, Royal Wulff or Royal Humpy, and the Red Quill, all in sizes 14 to 18. Midge imitations are good very early. Also try a Blue Winged Olive in sizes 18 and 20 when these tiny mayflies are on the water. Wet fly favorites are the Gold Ribbed Hare's Ear, Muskrat, Renegade, and Soft Hackle patterns in sizes 12 through 16. Lures include Mepps and Panther Martin.

Lake Estes

This 185-acre lake provides easy access and relaxed fishing for the entire family. Situated at Estes Park, it fishes best early and late in the season but offers year-round fishing as a portion of it stays free of ice throughout the winter. Boats are available to rent at the lake, and motors are allowed. For current angling details, it is best to check in at a local tackle shop. The lake is heavily fished and heavily stocked. Flyfishing is best during the evening.

ESTES PARK

The village of Estes Park, with its 5,000 year-round residents, is the threshold to Rocky Mountain National Park. Situated at 7,500 feet, Estes Park, although a destination ski area in winter, is really more oriented to catering to its many summer visitors. With tennis, swimming, two golf courses, horseback riding, boating, theatre, fishing, and hiking, this community is truly equipped to satisfy the interests of the entire family.

Camping, private and public, is available within minutes of downtown. A wide variety of lodging, from economical motels to guest ranches, is available, as is a broad spectrum of dining and shopping opportunities.

Next door to Estes Park is the 405 square miles of splendid scenery called Rocky Mountain National Park. It has two highway entrances, and in between is the famous Trail Ridge Road, straddling the continental divide at timberline, offering breathtaking views and the opportunity for spectacular photographs.

Encircled by high mountains, the village rarely experiences severe weather and expects to receive 300 days of sunshine throughout the year. This is a blessing to the estimated 3 million people who visit the park each year, as well as the passengers on the local aerial tramway, who enjoy panoramic views of distant mountain peaks.

Several festivals are featured each summer. They include Wildflower Music Festivals, the Rooftop Rodeo, Colorado Rocky Mountain Bluegrass Festival, Longs Peak Scottish Highland Festival, International Aspenfest, and the Alpine Bavarian Festival. These events make wonderful entertainment for the family and fisherman alike!

Camping

Public camping from the Estes Park area is in Rocky Mountain National Park. This famous park of 266,943 acres includes a thirty-five-mile chain of towering mountain peaks in the Never Summer Range and provides 200 nature trails, over 200 kinds of birds, and 700 species of wild flowers. With 107 peaks rising over 11,000 feet and fourteen over 13,000 feet, the park offers a broad range of outdoor activity, including fishing in many small streams and lakes.

There are four campgrounds on the east side of the park with 514 camping units. Two of these areas, Longs Peak and Aspenglen, are available on a first-come basis with 112 units. The other two, Moraine Park and Glacier Basin, have a total of 402 units, and are on the Ticketron Reservation System from the end of June through the middle of August. Reservations are made at: Ticketron Reservation Office, P.O. Box 2715, San Francisco, California 94126-2715. Some of the areas in the park are open year-round and some only during the summer.

Chamber of Commerce, Box 3050 CB 80517. Phone: 586-4431. 1-800-654-0949 in Colorado. 1-800-621-5888 outside Colorado.

Hospital/Ambulance: 586-2317.

Emergency: 911.

Rocky Mountain National Park: 586-2371.

Estes Park

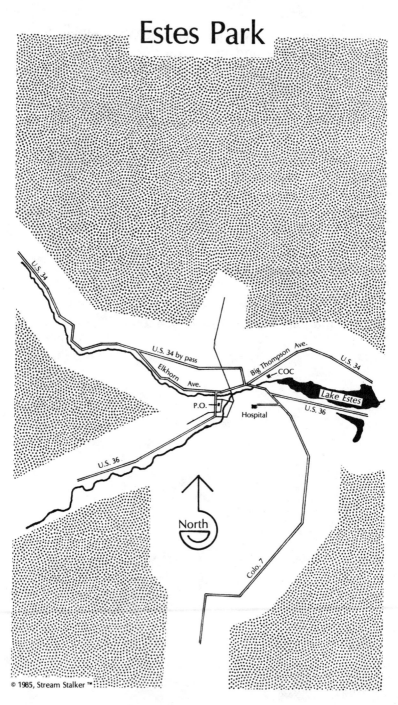

© 1985, Stream Stalker ™

134

RIO GRANDE RIVER

Map Reference 18 & 19

The Rio Grande River was referred to by the Spanish as the "Rio Grande del Norte"—the Big River of the North. Among these Spanish explorers searching for gold was Father Francisco Torres, who first saw and named the San Luis Valley. He was later wounded by Indians, and while watching the mountains to the east at sunset, he pointed to the range and cried, "Sangre de Cristo," indicating a vision of the blood of Christ. And so its name.

From the town of South Fork to the river's headwaters, there are forty-seven tributaries with 500 miles of stream to fish. A short distance below the Rio Grande Reservoir Dam the river enters a box canyon six miles in length, then flows out into an upland valley, where it meanders for nine miles. Fortunately, the river in these upper reaches is not dewatered for irrigation and does hold some nice fish.

From Creede down to Wagon Wheel Gap, there is a mixture of public access and private land—mostly the latter, so don't jump any fences, as you will most likely be on private property. A particularly long stretch of the river is on the Wason Ranch, located immediately above the bridge near Wagon Wheel Gap, where the river runs a couple hundred yards away from the road on the north side.

As you travel east through the basalt cliffs of the Gap, the river runs through a narrow canyon for about twelve miles to the town of South Fork. For the most part, the water

135

through here offers a wide variety of challenges to the angler. In the higher water, you will find a good bit of fast water running over boulders, creating chutes and pockets. The lower portion of this stretch slows down somewhat, and you will find more long runs and riffle/pool type water. The property adjacent to the river for this total distance is mostly open to the public. Dirt roads down to the river are frequent, and a few areas offer campsites. These accesses are obvious from the road.

Although access is not as convenient below South Fork as it is above, this is a popular area with anglers, and several state leases do allow some entrance to the river. The water here is considerably slower than above with a gradient of approximately ten feet per mile. The river starts to meander and pulls away from the highway. From here downstream you will encounter long runs and deep pools and a predominance of brown trout. The pines and firs of the upper river give way to cottonwoods as the river continues through Colorado's largest artesian basin, the San Luis Valley. Although irrigators do pull water from the river via the Famers Union Canal at Del Norte, they do consider the needs of anglers and try their best to maintain good minimum flows.

The river freezes over during winter, and ice-out usually occurs around mid-March. Runoff will start in May and will be heavy through June. Throughout this entire area, there are about one hundred miles of the river providing sport for the angler. The river is approximately 100 feet wide, and it is the second longest river in the United States, flowing 1,887 miles from its headwaters in the San Juan Mountains west of Creede to the Gulf of Mexico at Brownsville, Texas. Only the Missouri-Mississippi system is longer.

Throughout this watercourse, you may have the opportunity to sight golden and bald eagles, peregrine falcons, whooping cranes, and sandhill cranes in season. Driving west along the river, you will meet the foothills at the town of Del Norte. West of here, 96 percent of the Upper Rio Grande area is national forest land.

Although most of the fish hooked here will be brown

trout, there are populations of rainbows, brooks, and cutthroats. The browns reproduce very well in the Rio Grande and therefore dominate the fish population. According to reports from the Division of Wildlife, the resident populations of trout are growing larger and increasing in numbers in those areas with restricted fishing, and that is good news for all sport fishermen who enjoy this river.

This river is, of course, thought of as a trout river, but an extra added attraction can be found in the area between Monte Vista and Alamosa by fishing for northern pike. There is a fairly good population of these fish, and they will come to flies and lures in the slower water where weeds or obstructions offer them a place to hide. When flyfishing, use large streamers like Zonkers and Marabou Muddlers in bright colors. Don't forget to use a steel leader or fifty-pound nylon shock tippet to avoid being cut off when the fish strike.

Be sure to have a valid fishing license in this area, as the Wildlife Division representatives really do their duty on checking anglers. Fortunately, they do retain a sense of humor when performing this duty. One story tells the tale of a fisherman from New Mexico who, when asked for his Colorado license, responded that he had only a New Mexico license. Being taken back but for an instant, the officer smiled ever so slightly and replied calmly, "It takes a long line to reach New Mexico." He then issued the angler a summons!

In addition to the considerable public water above South Fork, several leases have been worked out between the Division of Wildlife and the ranchers along the river. These leases provide water availability to fishermen with the expectation that the property will be respected, so it is up to us as anglers to recognize our obligations and set good examples for future such negotiations on our behalf. The leases are well marked, and signs are posted to explain the boundaries of each.

Some rafting takes place on the water above South Fork, but it is fairly rough water, and hard-keel boats and canoes are not recommended. Most floating by raft or canoe takes place in the slower water below South Fork. Access is at the bridges on the state leases. Entry to and exit from the river are not necessarily convenient at all accesses, so if you plan to use a boat, scout the river ahead of time, and be sure that you put in and take out on public accesses. Bridges often used are the Granger Bridge and the State Bridge. For stillwater canoeing only minutes from South Fork, Beaver Creek and Big Meadows reservoirs are favorite destinations.

Tackle

For wading the Rio Grande, we certainly recommend felt-soled chest waders. Fly rods will range between size 6 and 8, depending on angling method and location in the river, and some of the local fishermen will use up to a size 10 when fishing the lower river for northern pike. This seems quite large but serves well when throwing large flies with heavy leaders to fish that love to get into the weeds. The spin fisherman will prefer to use line from four to six pounds.

Flies and Lures

An average assortment of Rocky Mountain fly patterns will do very well here, and the variety of insect life is a good mix of stoneflies, mayflies, and caddis flies. For dries, such patterns as Adams, Elk Hair Caddis, Humpies, and Irresistibles work very well. Attractor patterns like the Rio Grande King and Royal Wulff are very popular. The bigger flies seem to take the bigger fish here, so don't neglect throwing big, dark stonefly nymphs up near the bank. These large Pteronarcys imitations should be tied in sizes 2 to 6. Woolly Worms and Girdle Bugs are also effective. Favorite streamer patterns include Zonkers, Black

138

Matukas, Spruce Fly, and a local fly named Old Faithful, used in sizes 4 to 10. This fly has an olive chenille body, a wing feather taken from the top of a rump patch from a rooster pheasant, and the hackle is blue dun. For the spin fisherman, the Rapala No. 1 is a favorite along with Mepps and Panther Martin. Sometimes flyfishermen will try a tiny fly rod lure called a Fly Ike.

The main tributary to the Rio Grande is the South Fork, which enters the main river at—where else—South Fork! This small stream has good populations of trout with browns and rainbows in its lower reaches, and rainbows and brooks above Pass Creek. For about ten miles out of town, the highway follows the river, and flyfishing is good throughout the summer. There are large caddis fly hatches in late June and early July. Because the river is only about twenty feet wide, you can use smaller rods and lighter lines that you would use on the Rio Grande. Wading here can be done with hip boots, but on the Grande, be sure to wear felt-soled chest waders.

Lake Fishing

There are many lakes in the area accessible by car, four-wheel, or horseback with plenty of camping nearby. There are thirteen lakes within twenty minutes of South Fork, and inquiries should be made locally for details. Many of the lakes in the Upper Rio Grande area have a very good reputation for their rainbow and brook trout fishing and are, in fact, the reason many visitors vacation here. Two favorites are Continental Reservoir and Road Canyon Lake.

A lake of very easy access offering a variety of fish species is Homelake. It is located 1.9 miles east of the Monte Vista city limit, where you turn north and proceed one mile on County Road 3E. A gravel road follows the perimeter of the lake for about one mile. Fish here include bass, pike, and trout. Immediately to the north is a state wildlife nesting area for birds which is closed from February 15 to July 15.

CREEDE

What goes around, comes around, and that expression is well exemplified by the event that took place in 1892 when Robert Ford, "the man who shot Jesse James," was himself shot by a man named O'Kelly. The shotgun shooting took place in Ford's Exchange, a local saloon in Creede owned by Ford. Another well-known personality of the era was also a saloon manager and town marshall in Creede. His name was William Barclay "Bat" Masterson. By the year 1894, the population of this wild and unruly town on the Rio Grande was 10,000. As Calamity Jane dealt faro in a gambling hall, it was estimated that four out of ten people living in Creede in 1892 were either gunmen or fugitives from justice.

The town was named after N.C. Creede, who made the first important silver discovery at the Holy Moses Mine in 1889. Creede was the last of the great silver camps. Mining survived after the fall from the silver standard in 1893, with a resurgence during the 1960s and 1970s. Until 1985, the Homestake Mining Company still mined silver west of town on Bulldog Mountain. Old mines can be seen by driving up East and West Willow Creek canyons north of town. In a remote area east of Creede, visitors may hike to the spectacular limestone formations of the Wheeler Geologic Area.

Another good side trip by car is on the way toward Lake

City on Highway 149. Twenty-seven miles from town you can see North Clear Creek Falls, located about 100 feet off the highway.

At an elevation of 8,894 feet and with a population of 600, Creede's economic base is derived from cattle ranching, mining, and tourism. This is a very popular destination in the summer, offering over 500 miles of streams and fifty-two lakes. More than twenty guest ranches are located nearby, some offering horses and guide service for back-country pack trips. In the town itself are activities such as raft races between Creede and South Fork, church carnivals and bazaars, and from June to September the Creede Repertory Theatre performs most nights with several special events scheduled throughout the season. Public tennis courts are available, and the underground fire house provides a unique attraction for visitors.

A 6,900-foot blacktop air strip is situated one and one-half miles south of town.

Camping

On Highway 149, 12.1 miles southeast of Creede, is Palisade Campground. Located on the Rio Grande River, it offers thirteen sites with toilets and drinking water. This is a popular raft put-in point.

Southwest of town six miles on Highway 149, you will find Marshall Park Campground. As with other easily accessible campgrounds in the area, this one is heavily used. It has fifteen sites, toilets, and drinking water. Few trees and very little screening from highway traffic are available. The campground does have a rafting put-in point, plus there is fishing access to the Rio Grande River. This is the closest developed forest campground to Creede.

The next developed campground west of Creede is at 23.7 miles west on Highway 149. This is the South Clear Creek Falls Campground, with eleven units, drinking water, and toilets. There is also exposure to highway traffic, and there are few trees.

Several other camping areas are located on Forest Road 520. You will find this road off of Highway 149 at 20.1 miles southwest of Creede. These campgrounds—Crooked Creek, Road Canyon, River Hill, and Thirty Mile—offer a total of sixty-one units.

Chamber of Commerce: 658-2603.

Police: 658-2424.

Ambulance: 658-2211.

U.S. Forest Service, Box 270, Creede 81130. Phone: 658-2556.

Medical Clinic: 658-2416.

Creede

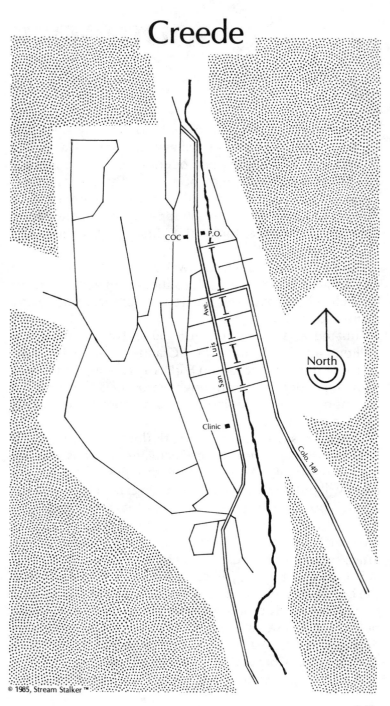

COC ■   ■ P.O.

Luis Ave.

San

Clinic ■

Colo. 149

North

SOUTH FORK

South Fork has been a logging community since the 1870s. It remains a lumber town with a major mill as well as several independent logging operations. In 1885 it was a railroad station, ranch, and "pop stop." There was no Wolf Creek Pass in those days. The town also served as a rendezvous point for traders, trappers, and Indians during the nineteenth century. The first post office was established in 1899.

During the first half of the twentieth century, the valley was busy with agricultural production of lettuce, peas, spinach, wheat, oats, and potatoes. There were also many cattle and sheep ranches.

Situated at an elevation of 8,250 feet with almost two million acres of the Rio Grande National Forest surrounding the area, South Fork is a growing community with expanded tourism, bright prospects for possible expansion of the ski industry, and continued nearby exploration for gold.

Due to its small size, South Fork does not offer a great deal in the way of recreational activities, but it is a center for good fishing. Within a short distance of town, easy hikes will put you into beautiful settings next to small lakes where you can fish, picnic, take photos, and just relax in the solitude of the mountains. Organized events in the area include raft races, rodeos, softball tournaments, artists' workshops, and flea markets.

Southwest of town, you can follow U.S. Highway 160 to the continental divide atop Wolf Creek Pass at an elevation of 10,850 feet. The pass was completed in 1916 with the help of Chinese laborers, and paving was completed during the Depression era with labor from the Civil Conservation Corps (CCC) and WPA crews.

Wagon Wheel Gap, west of South Fork, was important to

the development of its neighbor, Creede, first as a stage stop and later as a railroad station.

Camping

Several campgrounds are available within a short distance south between town and Wolf Creek Pass.

Lower and Upper Beaver Creek campgrounds: Within a half mile of each other, these two campgrounds are found by driving one mile southwest of town on Highway 160 to Forest Access Road 360 (Beaver Creek Road). Turn left and proceed 4.5 and 5 miles to the sites. They contain a total of thirty-three units. Both have toilets and drinking water. Fishing is handy in Beaver Creek and Beaver Creek Reservoir.

Cross Creek Campground: Beyond the above two areas another four miles is this campground with nine units and toilets, but no drinking water is available. South of the campground one-fourth mile, you will find the largest Douglas fir tree in the entire Rio Grande National Forest.

Highway Springs Campground: Located four miles southwest of town on Highway 160, this campground has eleven campsites, toilets, and parking for trailers and motorhomes. No drinking water is available.

Park Creek Campground: Travel southwest of town on Highway 160 for six and one-half miles and turn left into the campground, which is one-fourth mile west of the Park Creek Forest Road intersection. Thirteen campsites, toilets, and drinking water are available.

Big Meadows Campground: When you are twelve miles southwest of town on Highway 160, turn west on the Big Meadows access road. Proceed one and one-half miles to the campground, which has forty-three sites, toilets, and drinking water. Six sites are suitable for trailers. There is a boat ramp at Big Meadows Reservoir.

Ambulance: 873-5544.

Medical Clinic: 873-5846.

U.S. Forest Service, in Del Norte: 657-3321.

South Fork Business Association, Box 264, South Fork 81154. Phone: 873-5969.

River Notes

South Fork

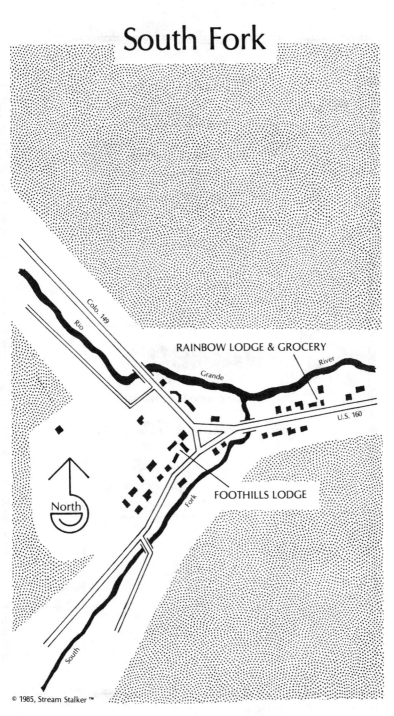

RAINBOW LODGE & GROCERY

FOOTHILLS LODGE

North

Colo. 149

Rio

Grande

River

U.S. 160

Fork

South

© 1985, Stream Stalker ™

South Fork

DEL NORTE

At 7,887 feet, Del Norte is located on the western edge of the San Luis Valley. It lies as a gateway to the San Juan Mountains and all the activities taking place there. The population of approximately 1,600 serves the needs of the ranching, mining, and lumbering industries in the surrounding area. Agriculture is the main economic factor in the region, and the low precipitation in this cool, dry climate requires that farms be irrigated to sustain the crops of hay, barley, and potatoes.

To the east is the Monte Vista Wildlife Refuge; to the west is South Fork and the historical mining town of Creede. Fishing and hunting are favorite outdoor activities in the area, and the visitor can do a good deal of sightseeing at the active ghost town of Summitville twenty-seven miles southwest of town, and at the nearby Wheeler Geological Area.

Activities available include tennis, camping, fishing, horseback riding, rafting, balloon rides, arrowhead hunting at Indian Head Peak, and scenic drives.

Camping

Cathedral Campground: From the Forest Service Ranger Station in town, travel 8.7 miles west on Highway 160 to the Embargo Creek Forest Access Road. Proceed twelve miles north to the campground. Located in an aspen grove, the area has twenty-nine campsites, drinking water, and toilets.

Chamber of Commerce, Box 148, Del Norte 81132. Phone: 657-2845.

U.S. Forest Service, 810 Grand Ave., Del Norte. Phone: 657-3321

Sheriff: 657-3933.

Del Norte

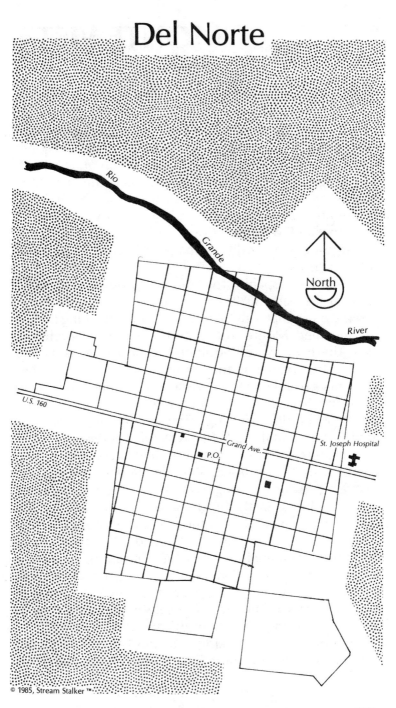

North

Rio
Grande

River

U.S. 160

Grand Ave.

P.O.

St. Joseph Hospital

151

MONTE VISTA

Flanked by the Sangre de Cristo Mountains to the east and the San Juan Mountains to the west, the city of Monte Vista lies on the Navajo Trail at an elevation of 7,666 feet. With a population of approximately 5,000, the economic activity of the community is strongest in the field of agriculture. Potatoes, wheat, and barley provide the main cash crops in Rio Grande County, of which Monte Vista is the largest city. In addition, many thousands of acres are put into crops of alfalfa, oats, hay, and vegetables.

Monte Vista (Spanish for "mountain view") was called Lariat in the early 1880s when the present town site was nothing more than a railroad siding with a watering tank. It was renamed Monte Vista when it was incorporated in 1886. The town is well equipped to host tourists, with a variety of services and attractions close by.

Six miles south of Monte Vista on Highway 15 is located the Monte Vista Wildlife Refuge, offering the visitor a wide range of birdlife viewing. This refuge is under the administration of the U.S. Fish & Wildlife Service as part of the Alamosa-Monte Vista National Wildlife Refuge Complex of the National Wildlife Refuge System. The program provides nesting, resting, and feeding areas for migratory birds. In the spring and fall you may see the almost extinct whooping crane flock. The whooper is one of the world's fifteen crane species and is North America's tallest bird, standing four to five feet with a wing span of up to seven feet. More common sightings include egrets, gulls, terns, avocets, herons, snipes, and in early October, thousands of sandhill cranes. A self-guided loop drive is open daily during winter, spring, and summer.

Another trip worth taking is to the Great Sand Dunes National Monument, approximately forty miles to the east of town.

In town, facilities are available for bowling, swimming, picnicking, and tennis. A nine-hole golf course is open to the public from spring through fall. Throughout the summer, special events include raft races, fairs, and the Ski-Hi Stampede Rodeo, the oldest in Colorado.

Camping

Rock Creek Campground: From Monte Vista, go two miles south on Highway 15. Turn west onto Rock Creek Road and continue to the Forest Service boundary, where it becomes Forest Road 265. The campground is sixteen miles southwest of Highway 15. There are fourteen campsites, toilets, no drinking water, and spaces for trailers. Firewood availability is limited.

Alamosa Campground: Drive twelve miles south of town on Highway 15. Turn west onto Twelve Mile Road and follow it west to the forest boundary, where the road becomes Alamosa-Conejos River Road 250. The campground is twelve miles west of Highway 15. There are ten campsites, toilets, drinking water, and limited firewood. It is difficult to maneuver trailers in this campground.

Chamber of Commerce, 25 Park (Grand) Ave. 81144. Phone: 852-2731.

Ambulance: 852-5111.

Community Hospital, 95 W. 1st Ave. Phone: 852-3541.

Alamosa-Monte Vista National Wildlife Refuge, Box 1148, Alamosa 81101. Phone: 589-4021.

Monte Vista

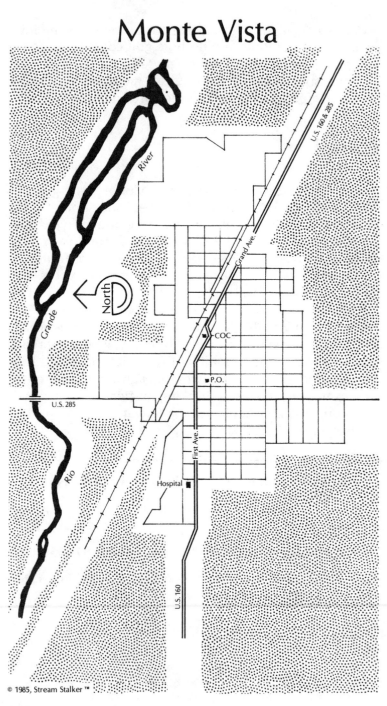

ALAMOSA

As your car rolls effortlessly down the south side of Poncha Pass near Salida, you enter the largest alpine valley in the world. As you travel through this hundred-mile-long, fifty-mile-wide valley, you'll enjoy the beauty of the San Juan Mountains to the west and the Sangre de Cristo Range to the east. In the center of this vast plain is the city of Alamosa—the commercial, medical, and educational hub of the San Luis Valley. Settled in 1878 on the Rio Grande River, the town was named for the many trees that lined the river's banks. Alamosa in Spanish means cottonwood.

Until 1860, this part of Colorado was actually in New Mexico. Fort Garland, to the east of town, was in 1858 the northernmost army post in New Mexico and was established to protect the settlers in the San Luis Valley. This restored fort was the last command of Colonel Kit Carson in 1867. It was abandoned in 1883. Also to the east of town is San Luis, Colorado's oldest town, founded in 1851.

With a population of nearly 7,000 and at an elevation of 7,500 feet, Alamosa is the home of Adams State College. Along with its normal function of educating students, the college also adds a cultural facet to this agricultural support community. In addition to cattle and sheep ranches, agriculture is the mainstay of the valley, with potatoes and lettuce being the main crops.

Community events include rodeos, art shows, and hot air balloon rallies. In addition to the angling opportunities in the valley, other recreational activities include a municipal golf course and a natural artesian warm-water swimming pool.

Two special points of interest attract visitors to this community. The first is the 9,186-acre Alamosa Wildlife

Refuge, known for its wide variety of migratory bird life. The refuge is located five miles from Highway 160 and 17 East. Information can be obtained at refuge headquarters.

The other popular area is Great Sand Dunes National Monument, located thirty-two miles northeast of Alamosa. For 15,000 years the dunes have been formed by a natural trap in the Sangre de Cristo Mountains, allowing the ever-shifting sand to rise as high as 700 feet above the floor of the valley to cover a total area of over 150 square miles. The main dune field covers fifty square miles. Eighty-eight campsites are available within the fifty-seven-square-mile monument. There are no hook-ups, but drinking water and restrooms are available.

Activities at the monument include a nature trail, backpacking areas, a visitor center that is open every day except Christmas, children's programs, moonlight walks, and evening campfire programs. The best time to visit is in the morning or evening, as midday summer temperatures are uncomfortable.

Alamosa Chamber of Commerce, Cole Park, Alamosa 81101. Phone: 589-6531

Police: 589-2548

Alamosa-Monte Vista National Wildlife Refuge, Box 1148, Alamosa. Phone: 589-4021.

Great Sand Dunes National Monument, Mosca CO 81146. Phone: 378-2312.

Alamosa Community Hospital: 589-2511

Alamosa

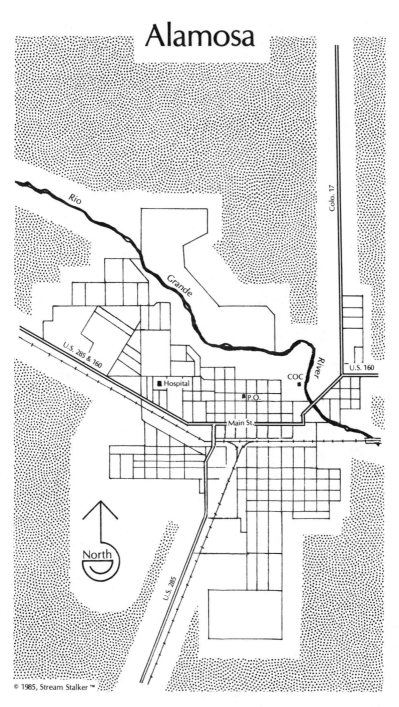

River Notes

ROARING FORK RIVER

The Roaring Fork River can be considered one of reward and challenge to all anglers who wade its cold waters. From its headwaters on 12,095-foot Independence Pass, downstream twenty miles to its entrance into the town of Aspen, the river flows with increasing volume and contains fish primarily in the six- to twelve-inch class. The largest of them are closer to town, where the volume is greater and the holding water is deeper. Browns, rainbows, and brook trout will be found here, and although much of the river flows through national forest land, some private property is involved and must be respected.

The "Fork" flows through a canyon from Aspen down to the Upper Woody Creek Bridge, a distance of six miles. This stretch of river is relatively swift and boulder strewn, but holds a good population of fish and is open to the public for its entire length. This reach is designated Wild Trout water, is controlled by regulations limiting fishing to flies only, and all fish must be returned to the river. Access in town is from the Slaughterhouse Bridge on Cemetery Lane at the very west edge of town. Turn north at the stoplight on Highway 82 next to the golf course. Drive 1.1 miles, and you will find parking at the bridge. Most anglers will walk downstream and fish back to their car, but you can also fish upstream toward town. A former railroad bed, and currently a hiking/biking path, makes access to the water very convenient.

Entrance to the river at the lower end of the canyon is at the Upper Woody Creek Bridge. The turnoff from Highway 82 is at the Woody Creek Canyon sign approximately six miles west of Aspen. Parking is available along the road near the bridge. Most anglers will wade/walk upstream from this access. Although close to town, this six-mile strech of river is not overfished. Trout are abundant here and will be taken more often on nymphs than dry flies, although evening dry fly fishing in July and August can be outstanding. Water speed here is approximately four feet per second, with a lot of boulders in the river making pocket fishing the order of the day.

From the Upper Woody Creek Bridge downstream to Basalt, the river flows through a somewhat wider valley floor. Although shallower on the whole, the river is still fast, and wading must be done with care. Access is from pullouts off Highway 82, and these are numerous and apparent as one drives the road. Stretches of private property do exist, but public water is abundant. The trout between Aspen and Basalt will average about eleven inches. Fish sixteen to eighteen inches are caught often, and those of this size are more common in the canyon above the Woody Creek Bridge as they have better holding water and less fishing pressure.

For about one mile immediately below Basalt there is good access to the Roaring Fork directly off Highway 82. Good runs and pools hold a fair number of trout even with the above-average pressure they receive. One will also start to catch Rocky Mountain whitefish from here downstream to the confluence with the Colorado River at Glenwood Springs. Though not as active as trout after being hooked, whitefish can provide action to supplement the trout and will take flies just as readily as trout.

Because the Frying Pan River enters the Fork at Basalt, the river now takes on larger proportions. The water is somewhat slower due to less gradient, and the added volume makes the river deeper. Fewer places to cross the river will be found where access is available, but less access is available due to private property. Without a raft to float the m. , there is very little access to the lower twenty miles of the Roaring Fork from Basalt to Glenwood Springs.

Between Basalt and Carbondale there are only four public access points. The first is the one-mile reach downstream from Basalt. The second is found driving west, at 2.1 miles from the highway stoplight in Basalt, and turning left on the road that angles off Highway 82. Drive .9 miles further and park along the road, or pull into the commercial development on the right. At this point, entrances to the river will be obvious. The third access is at Catherine Store. After driving west 7.5 miles from the Basalt stoplight, turn left (south) next to the store. Within one-half mile, you will be able to park at the bridge. You can then walk upstream along the railroad tracks, but don't fish downstream of the bridge, as this is private property.

The last place to enter the river is immediately above the bridge over Highway 133 going to Carbondale. The parking area is reached from the eastbound (toward Aspen) lane only, as this is a divided highway. About fifty yards upstream of the highway intersection, a small turnout will be evident. Turn off here and drive to the bottom of the hill on a rough dirt road. Use caution if wet. Wade only the north half of the river, as the south half is private with no permission granted. You can fish up past the irrigation intake for a short distance before coming to private property.

The access points to the Fork between Carbondale and Glenwood Springs are few and really do not put you into good stretches of river because either the water is quite heavy or mobility along the bank is difficult. Driving west on Highway 82 for 1.2 miles beyond the intersection of Highway 133, turn left onto a narrow blacktop road, cross a cattle guard, and continue 0.3 miles to the Sutank Bridge over the Fork. This is one of the accesses.

Further downstream is another access gained through a lease agreement between the land owner and the Division of Wildlife. From the Highway 133 intersection, drive west 3.8 miles to the Cattle Creek turnoff to the right. The road sign here indicates the road to the right goes to

Cottonwood Pass and Gypsum. You want to make a U turn here to the left so you are going back east. Proceed 1.2 miles and angle off the highway on a ranch access road. Almost immediately you will turn right, cross the railroad tracks, and read a sign stating the river here is state-stocked, fishermen are welcome, and respect your privilege. For permission to park and fish, inquire at the white house at the end of the lane. You will find some water here that is easy to get to and provides some long runs and interesting riffles.

Fishing is also available from downtown Glenwood Springs by entering the river through the Kiwanis Park on the west side of the river. This park is located within 200 yards of the confluence with the Colorado River and can be found by crossing over the Roaring Fork on the one-way, 7th Avenue Bridge and turning left at the first intersection. This section of the Roaring Fork Valley below Carbondale is interesting because of the series of sloping stream terraces that characterize its floor and flanks. The oldest terrace is almost 800 feet above the present valley floor. At least six steps to the level of the river exist, representing six ancient floodplains. Each is a remnant of a former valley floor.

The Roaring Fork has a wide variety of aquatic insect life in very abundant quantities. Pteronarcys californica is the dominant stonefly, and it hatches from late May to early June with emergence at Carbondale usually on Memorial Day. Other smaller stoneflies emerge throughout the summer, and fishing nymphal imitations is very effective. Caddis flies would head the list for sheer numbers of insects. Starting in May they hatch throughout the summer and into fall. Their size varies from 10 to 20, with No. 14 being most common. Colors vary from pale tan to almost black. Mayflies are also abundant in a wide range of sizes and colors and are particularly noticeable in the evenings.

Wading the Fork is usually difficult due to the size and roundness of riverbed rocks. Metal cleats are helpful all year, particularly in the lower river and/or late in the season. Chest waders are definitely recommended anywhere below Aspen.

Tackle

For flyfishing lines, sizes 4 through 6 from Aspen to Basalt. Use sizes 5 through 7 from Basalt to Glenwood Springs. Floating lines are suitable to all fishing, although sinking tips could be used in the lower river if streamer fishing.

Flies and Lures

Dry flies—Adams, Lt. Cahill, Elk Hair Caddis, Royal Wulff, Yellow Humpy, Irresistible, all in sizes 14 to 18.

Nymphs and wets—Gold Ribbed Hare's Ear, Renegade, Muskrat, Western Coachman, and Rio Grande King, all in sizes 10 to 16. Brown and black stonefly nymphs, Brown Hackle Peacock, and assorted Woolly Worms in sizes 4 to 8.

Streamers—more effective in the lower river below Basalt than above. Muddler Minnow, Matuka (brown, black, olive), Light and Dark Spruce Fly, Sculpin, all in sizes 2 to 6.

Terrestrials—Hoppers (brown, yellow, green), ants (black and rusty in sizes 16 to 20).

River Notes

FRYING PAN RIVER

Legend has it that two mountain men were attacked by Utes while trapping beaver on this river. One was seriously wounded, so his partner left him in a cave by the river and went for help, hanging a frying pan visibly in a nearby tree to mark the location of the cave. When he returned with soldiers, the frying pan helped him locate his friend, who unfortunately had not survived his wounds. Thus the river was named.

Water from the headwaters of the river is funneled into the Boustead and Carlton tunnels beneath the continental divide to be delivered to the Arkansas River as part of the Fryingpan-Arkansas Water Diversion Project. Between Ruedi Reservoir and the town of Basalt is one of the most scenic valleys in Colorado. Its entire length is cut into the Red Beds of sandstone and shale, contrasting beautifully with the green hillsides of the area. Boulders from the gray and black volcanic rock on the lava-capped mesa north of town inspired the name of the town of Basalt which lies at the confluence of the Frying Pan and Roaring Fork rivers.

The drive from Basalt to the Ruedi Dam covers fourteen miles. The total trip might take twenty-five minutes driving time if your only intent is to "get there." If you were to stop and enjoy the scenery, the trip could take an hour. If you wanted to fish your way up this length of the Frying Pan River, you might spend two weeks working your way

165

upstream. Fishing could begin in the town of Basalt at the confluence with the Roaring Fork River, and with few exceptions, you could wade and fish the entire fourteen miles of river. Pool/riffle sequences are plentiful here between the banks of the forty-foot-wide stream channel. The "Pan" runs cold due to bottom releases from the dam, with temperature extremes from about 39 to 50 degrees F.

Prolific mayfly and caddis hatches, combined with special method and harvest regulations and easy access make this river one of the most popular in Colorado. With normal snowpack and controlled discharge from the dam, the Pan can be fishable in May, June, and July when other streams might be high and roily.

The valley is sparsely populated, the road is paved, the scenery is beautiful, and the fish population is large. It includes rainbows, browns, brook trout, and an occasional cutthroat, with twelve- to sixteen-inch fish common.

Occasionally, the lower four miles of the river will run dirty due to snowmelt or heavy rain in the area of the red sandstone formations called the "Seven Castles." Usually the Pan above this area will be clear.

Behind Ruedi Dam is the reservoir of the same name. Boats are not available for rent, so to fish here you need your own boat, or do your casting from shore. The inlet of the Frying Pan is one of the more popular areas to fish. The Pan above the reservoir offers stream fishing in water considerably faster than below it. Roadside fishing is available up to Chapman Reservoir, six miles from Ruedi. Chapman is a small impoundment fishable from the bank or your own small craft or belly-boat. Camping is also available here. Fish are small but plentiful.

Because of its quality, the Pan below Ruedi Reservoir receives the most angling attention. The road is adjacent to the river for essentially the entire fourteen miles. Pullouts for parking are numerous, and there are very few stretches of private property. These are marked, and should be respected.

Insects

Although Pteronarcys and Acroneuria stoneflies were once in abundance in the Pan, the cold outflows from Ruedi Dam have eliminated them. Wonderful hatches of midges, caddis flies, and mayflies, however, keep the angler and the fish plenty busy during the summer months. Midges by the millions dominate the water immediately below the dam. Brachycentrus, Hydropsyche, and Rhyacophila caddis are in great abundance, as are Cloeon, Cinigula, Baetis, and Ephemerella mayflies. Of particular importance is the Ephemerella glacialis, a size No. 10 to No. 12 "Green Drake" that hatches in July and August and turns the heads of all trout in the river.

Wading

The Pan presents few difficulties in wading compared to most Colorado rivers. The rocks of the riverbed are more angular than round, and in most areas they do not collect slippery growths of algae.

Tackle

Fly Equipment: Number 4 and 5 lines will do the trick on the entire river. Floating lines only.

Flies and Lures

Dry—Adams, downwing caddis patterns with brown, olive, or tan bodies, Blue Wing Olive, Midge imitations, Blue Dun and Blue Quill, Red Quill—all of these in size No. 14 to 18 with the midges down to 24. Also a Green Drake imitation in No. 10 or 12.

Nymph and Wet—Green Caddis Larvae, Gold Ribbed Hare's Ear, Muskrat, Renegade, Pheasant Tail Nymph, Olive Scud, Brown Hackle Peacock—all in sizes 14 to 18. Also, some midge larvae and pupae down to No. 24. Attractors such as Western Coachman and Rio Grande King in No. 12 and 14 can be good.

Streamers—Not used extensively, but occasionally a Grey Ghost, Muddler Minnow, Spruce Fly in sizes 6 and 8 can be effective.

Terrestrials—Black ants, Hoppers, and occasional leaf hoppers.

Because nearly all fish are returned to the water on this river, most fishing is done with fly tackle, but spin fishing can be effective on occasion. It is done most often with a bubble and a wet fly, or with small gold or silver lures such as Mepps, Panther Martin, and Colorado Spinners.

Tributaries

Nine miles east of Aspen, about halfway to the summit of Independence Pass, is Lincoln Creek. Small and relatively fast, this creek is paralleled by a dirt road six miles to Grizzly Reservoir. We do not recommend driving a standard sedan to the reservoir, but a vehicle with somewhat higher clearance is no problem. Both reservoir and creek contain trout—primarily rainbows—in the seven to twelve-inch range. Water demands on the Eastern Slope dictate flows in Lincoln Creek, but it is usually fishable from mid-July. Several campgrounds are situated along Highway 82 in this vicinity.

As the Fork passes through Aspen, it picks up the flows of Hunter Creek, Castle Creek, and Maroon Creek. These are all fishable tributaries, but they are relatively small and fast and fish better with fly tackle than with spin gear. Hunter Creek is accessible by hiking from town for about two miles. The stream can then be followed for several more miles with the prospect of fishing to large numbers of small brook trout. These fish so overpopulate the stream that special regulations are in effect to encourage their harvest.

Castle Creek is fishable from its upper reaches at the ghost town of Ashcroft. It is paralleled for this twelve-mile distance by a paved road and public access is alternated with private property. Small rainbows will be the predominant fish caught here. The Castle Creek Valley is beautiful, the ghost town interesting, and all visitors should at least make the drive a part of the Aspen vacation.

In the next valley west lies Maroon Creek, which has characteristics almost identical to Castle Creek. Relatively small and fast, the creek is best fished with fly equipment. During the peak tourist season of July 1 through Labor Day, the Forest Service runs shuttle buses up this valley to help protect the environment from the adverse effects of auto traffic. Maroon Lake headwaters the creek, and its backdrop of the Maroon Bells (both peaks over 14,000 feet) make it Colorado's most photographed natural attraction. You can drive your vehicle to the Aspen Highlands Ski Area parking lot to meet the bus, enjoy the ride up the valley, picnic or fish the lake during the day, and return on another bus later in the day. The buses operate each half hour from 9 a.m. to 5 p.m., and a nominal fee is charged. Before 9 and after 5, personal cars may be driven to the lake. Camping is also available on a first-come basis and permits for camping are issued at the entrance station on the road. An interesting attraction of the lake aside from its natural beauty is the stick and mud, multi-roomed beaver lodge. The entrance is under water, and dry rooms are reached through a tunnel rising to above water level inside.

Below the Carbondale Bridge, the Crystal River enters the Roaring Fork from the south. The valley of the Crystal River should be driven if only to see its beauty. Starting at

Carbondale with the massive Mount Sopris as a landmark, the drive through red shale and sandstone glaciated slopes along the river to the town of Marble will be worth the journey, even if you do not stop to fish the river. Pieces of white marble can be seen strewn along the banks of the river, where much of it was placed years ago to prevent erosion of the riverbanks. This marble was taken from nearby quarries.

Attractive as it appears as a trout stream, the river is not considered an important source of angling pleasure. The few resident fish in the river are small and infrequent because of the adverse effects of coal silt coming down Coal Creek into the Crystal.

Wading in any of these tributaries poses no problem because they are small and easily fished without stepping into the water very far. The main consideration is the swiftness of the current in some places.

Standard fly patterns usually work well in these small streams, because many of the fish are stocked and are not quite as selective as those wild fish of the larger streams.

ASPEN

Before discovery by the white man, the Aspen area was the home of the Utah Indians (Utes). In 1874, Dr. F.V. Hayden, a U.S. geologist, and his party mapped this area. Independence Pass (on the continental divide) was a boundary between Indian and white land. When gold was discovered at the town of Independence in 1879, the white man pushed across the divide and started to settle the Roaring Fork Valley. The Roaring Fork River was named by Charles Bennett in 1879, and his party named the new city at the foot of Aspen Mountain "Ute City." A year later the name was changed to Aspen, and by 1884, the town had a population of 6,000.

To the east of Aspen thirteen miles lie the decaying ruins of the Independence town site. Considered the first mining camp in the Aspen area, the first gold was found on July 4, 1879, and the town was named in honor of the day. At one time it was also known as Chipita, for the wife of Chief Ouray. By 1882, the camp contained over forty businesses and reached a population of nearly 2,000. Room and board at the Independence House was two dollars per day. Mining became less and less prosperous, and by 1888 the population was fewer than 100.

Independence Pass, the route to the town of Independence, was an old Indian trail used later by trail riders when Aspen began to boom. The first rough wagon road was built over the pass in 1881 at the elevation of 12,095 feet and is now one of the highest paved roads in the United States.

Aspen itself was founded by prospectors in 1879. Its boom came when it was served on the "Silver Circuit" by the narrow gauge Denver & Rio Grande Railroad and the broad gauge Colorado Midland Railroad, which arrived in Aspen in 1887 and 1888, respectively. The town grew with silver mining to 15,000 residents, and in 1892 it was considered the world's richest silver-producing community, with an annual silver ore production amounting to $10 million. The following year, silver was demonetized, and the population started its exodus to find work in gold camps. From a peak population of 15,000, Aspen dropped to 700 in the 1920s. After World War II members of the Tenth Mountain Division returned to Aspen and started the ski industry which today has grown to the most famous in the world.

The former town of Ashcroft lies ten miles from Highway 82 up Castle Creek Valley. Silver was discovered here in 1879, and it was considered a boom town in 1882. By 1885, the summer population was 2,500 and the town boasted among other things a bowling alley, six hotels, and seventeen saloons. The railroads went to Aspen and not Ashcroft in 1887, and the town died by 1900, leaving it as it is today—a ghost town. Due to its natural beauty, several movies have been filmed here and in the Castle Creek Valley.

Aspen today truly deserves its standing as the country's best-known alpine resort. At an elevation of almost 8,000 feet, this town offers activity in such abundance that a summer vacation here is usually too short no matter how long the vacation might be! Sports, culture, recreation, shopping, and sightseeing are what Aspen is all about during the summer.

The town has no shortage of activities for the tourist. The brick paved pedestrian mall downtown is the center for shopping opportunities in a wide variety of shops, while impromptu music is performed by students of the Aspen Music Festival. A block away, spectators are cheering their adopted softball team in Wagner Park. While some visitors are making arrangements for raft trips and hot air balloon trips, others are enjoying tennis or golf in the high-country sunshine. Jeep trips, concerts, rodeos, wind-surfing, chairlift rides, mine tours, nature tours at the Aspen Center for Environmental Studies, ballet, theatre, lectures, etc. are all available for the visitor's enjoyment during the summer. All this in addition to fine fishing!

Life is casual in Aspen, and shorts and T-shirts are most common during the day, with trousers and sweater more appropriate in the evening. None of Aspen's many fine restaurants requires a tie!

Ten miles to the southwest of Aspen is the well-known ski resort of Snowmass. This year-round recreation center provides the tourist with a variety of lodging, restaurants, a health club, an eighteen-hole championship caliber golf course complementing the one at Aspen, tennis, swimming, and many other activities. Many special events take place here, including theatre, music, and sports.

Surrounding the Aspen/Snowmass area are 2 million acres of the White River National Forest, established in 1891. It has 1,377 miles of roads and trails and is home to 20,000 elk, making it one of the largest herds on the continent.

Camping

There are five campgrounds between Aspen and the summit of Independence Pass. These include Difficult, Weller, and Lostman along Highway 82, plus Lincoln Gulch and Portal along the Lincoln Creek Road. This road is not maintained, and driving to Portal is not recommended in a standard sedan. These five campgrounds provide a total of eighty units.

From Aspen south along the Maroon Creek Road to Maroon Lake you will find four campgrounds. The largest is at the lake with forty-three units, plus Silver Bar, Silver Bell, and Silver Queen along this road with a total of fourteen units. For anyone interested in hiking, there are over 100 miles of trails at elevations from 9,000 to 14,000 feet in the Maroon Bells-Snowmass Wilderness Area.

During the day in summer, personal vehicle traffic to Maroon Lake is not allowed, as the Forest Service provides bus transportation to relieve impacts on the valley from excessive traffic. Personal cars may make the trip in early morning and again in the evening. Inquiries concerning this procedure may be obtained at the Forest Service office or at the checkpoint along the Maroon Creek road at the Aspen Highlands Ski Area.

Aspen Resort Association, 303 E. Main St. 81611. Phone: 925-1940.

Emergency: 911.

Police: 925-2025.

U.S. Forest Service, 806 W. Hallam, Aspen. Phone: 925-3445.

Aspen

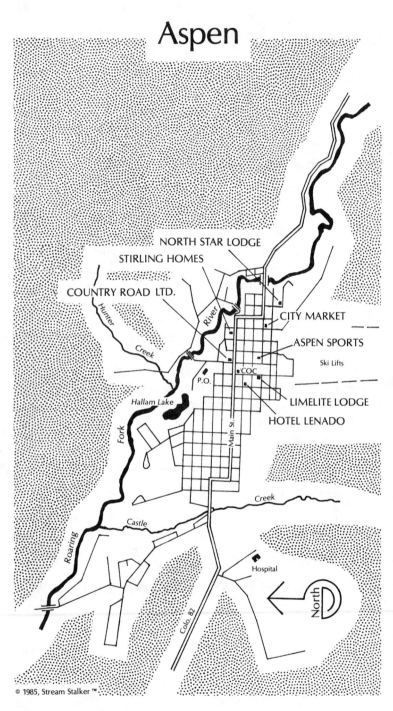

NORTH STAR LODGE
STIRLING HOMES
COUNTRY ROAD LTD.
CITY MARKET
ASPEN SPORTS
Ski Lifts
COC
P.O.
LIMELITE LODGE
HOTEL LENADO
Hallam Lake
Hunter
Creek
River
Main St.
Fork
Roaring
Castle
Creek
Hospital
North
Colo. 82

Aspen

175

176

Snowmass Village

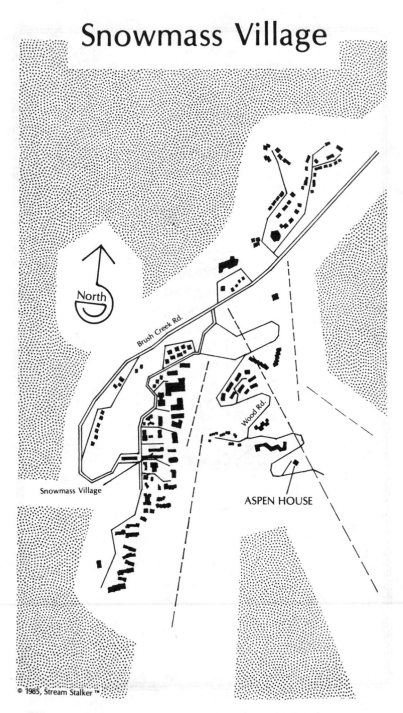

North

Brush Creek Rd.

Wood Rd.

Snowmass Village

ASPEN HOUSE

© 1985, Stream Stalker™

Snowmass Village

BASALT

Originally a wild and wooly railroad town in the 1880s supporting the silver mining activities at Aspen, Basalt is now a small community thoroughly accustomed to seeing fishermen walking through town in waders. The town provides all the basic needs of the serious angler—lodging, groceries, restaurants, and tackle shops. The Roaring Fork and Frying Pan rivers are considered two of the finest fly fishing streams in Colorado, and Basalt is at their confluence.

For the person staying here, fishing is literally within walking distance of the motels. For those wishing to camp, services are available close to town, and tent camping is allowed at Ruedi Reservoir, only fourteen miles from town. Ruedi offers fishing, water skiing, and sailboarding.

Although possibilities for night-life and family entertainment are limited in Basalt, a pleasant drive of eighteen miles allows you to enjoy the many services and activities of world-famous Aspen. Athletic, outdoor, and cultural events cover a broad spectrum in Aspen in summer.

Basalt is low-key, comfortable, and at the center of some of Colorado's finest fishing. Lakes and streams abound in the area and offer enough water and angling variety to fill an entire vacation.

Camping

To camp out of the Basalt area, drive east on the Frying Pan River road. Six campgrounds are available from fourteen to twenty-eight miles from town. Three campgrounds are located fourteen miles from Basalt, just beyond the Ruedi Dam, by turning right at the Ruedi Boat

Ramp sign. Here, you will find Mollie B, Little Maud, and Little Mattie campgrounds with a total of sixty-seven campsites. Water, restrooms, and a boat launch area are available.

Beyond Basalt twenty-two miles, at the very eastern end of Ruedi Reservoir, is Dearhammer Campground with thirteen campsites, toilets, and drinking water. On the North Fork of the Frying Pan River, twenty-six miles from town, is Elk Wallow Campground, providing seven campsites. Staying on the blacktop road along the main river at mile twenty-eight is Chapman Dam Campground. It contains thirty-three campsites with drinking water, toilets, and fishing available on the river as well as the small reservoir.

Town Hall: 927-4701

Forest Service Office (in Carbondale), 620 Main Street 81623. Phone: 963-2266.

Basalt

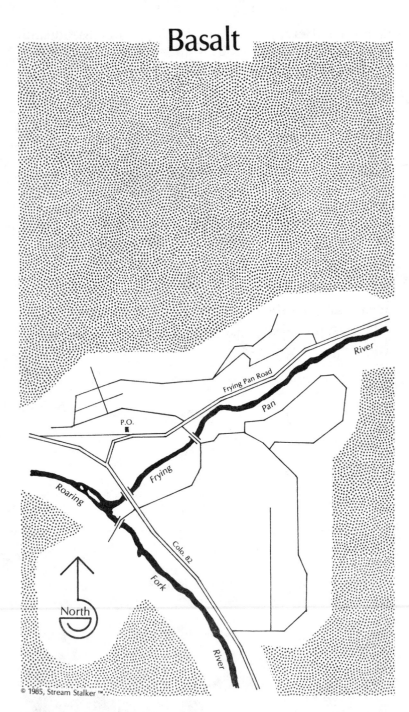

P.O.

Frying Pan Road

River

Pan

Frying

Roaring

Colo. 82

Fork

River

North

© 1985, Stream Stalker ™.

CARBONDALE

For miles in all directions, the landmark of Mount Sopris is an imposing sight. Its 12,953 height rises 6,000 feet above the valley floor. The mountain was named after explorer Captain Richard Sopris, the first white man to visit the Roaring Fork Valley. In the shadow of this dominant natural structure lies the small community of Carbondale at an elevation of 6,200 feet. The economic base here is derived from the coal mining near Redstone, from agricultural support, and from tourism. The downtown section consists essentially of one street (Main Street), which is supplemented by two shopping centers on Highway 133. Most of the recreational opportunities are located either up or down the Roaring Fork Valley, but the town does offer a public swimming pool, lodging, interesting shops, and restaurants.

Just one mile south of town on Highway 133 is the Crystal River Rearing Ponds. Visitors to this Colorado Division of Wildlife facility are welcome to tour the grounds and view some of the thousands of trout that are released to Colorado waters each year.

Eighteen miles south of Carbondale is the very small community of Redstone. Listed as a National Historic Site, this town on the Crystal River offers shopping, sightseeing, and the Redstone Museum, highlighting the area's coal mining history. The town was founded by J.G. Osgood, who built a forty-two-room manor house, a forty-room inn, and a model village for his employees. Osgood's Crystal River mansion, *Cleveholm*, is a Tudor Castle.

Up the road a few miles from Redstone is the town of Marble. In its day, this community produced the fine white marble from the Yule and Strauss quarries. The largest single block of marble ever quarried in the world came from here. The block weighed one hundred tons and now marks the Tomb of the Unknown Soldier in Arlington Cemetery. Marble from this site was also used in the Colorado state capitol and the Lincoln Memorial. Because of the development of marble substitutes, the quarries no longer operate.

Camping

South from Carbondale on Highway 133, four campgrounds are available. Twelve miles from town, turn east along Avalanche Creek. Continue one-half mile and three miles, respectively, to reach Janeway Campground with ten units and Avalanche Campground with nine units. Toilets, but no drinking water, are available at either site. The latter provides trailhead parking for the Avalanche Creek Trail.

The Redstone Campground is fifteen and one-half miles south on 133 and provides twenty-four campsites with drinking water and toilets. At twenty-two miles south, having turned left at the bottom of McClure Pass onto the road to Marble, you will find Bogan Flats Campground, with thirty-four units, toilets, and drinking water.

U.S. Forest Service, 620 Main St., Carbondale 81623. Phone: 963-2266.

Ambulance: 963-2235.

Chamber of Commerce, 256 Main St. Phone: 963-1890.

Carbondale

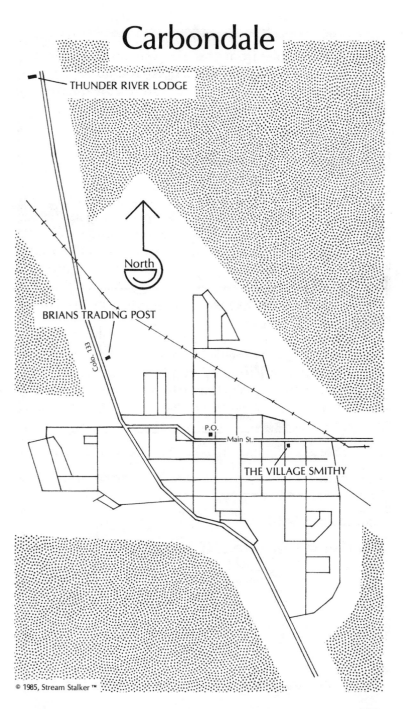

THUNDER RIVER LODGE

North

BRIANS TRADING POST

Colo. 133

P.O.

Main St.

THE VILLAGE SMITHY

© 1985, Stream Stalker ™

Carbondale

Thunder River Lodge

0179 Hwy 133   963-2543

HWY JCT 133 & 82, CARBONDALE
CLEAN MODERN UNITS • COLOR CABLE TV
YEAR ROUND SPORTS
SKI - FISH - HUNT - HIKE
REASONABLE RATES

GLENWOOD SPRINGS

This Western Slope community grew from the remnants of Fort Defiance, a blockhouse built for protection from the Ute Indians about six miles northwest of the present town site. Founded in 1882, this town was incorporated in 1885. The town was named by Isaac Cooper, an early visitor to the area, after his home town of Glenwood, Iowa. One of the city's early celebrities was famous for the part he played with the Earp brothers in the gunfight at the O.K. Corral in Tombstone, Arizona. His name was John "Doc" Holliday, who died in 1887 at the age of thirty-five and is buried in Glenwood Springs.

The most famous attraction of the town is the hot springs pool. At two blocks in length, the pool is the world's largest natural warm mineral water open air pool. It draws swimmers and soakers from up and down the valley in both summer and winter. In the early days the springs were considered by the Utes as big medicine. They used the springs in an annual religious rite because they believed that the waters had sacred curing properties and would make them more skillful warriors and hunters. Aspen millionaire Walter Devereux backed and developed the construction of the 500-foot-long pool as well as the hotel that overlooks it. He wished to offer a resort area to the mining field workers of the Western Slope. The pool is maintained at a temperature of 90 degrees F. and has an Olympic diving facility, lap lanes, a water slide, a therapy pool, and a kiddie pool.

Glenwood Springs is situated at the confluence of the Roaring Fork and Colorado rivers at an elevation of 5,747 feet. The town offers a variety of activities for the visitor, including raft trips in spring and early summer, hiking trails, two parks, tennis courts, and two golf courses.

A nice auto trip involves a drive east through sixteen

miles of sheer canyon walls of the Glenwood Canyon flanking the Colorado River. This area is very popular with kayakers and rafters. For a good hiking experience, you can stop at a rest area about a mile east of the Shoshone Power Plant in the canyon and take the trail to Hanging Lake. The trail is slightly over a mile long and is quite steep, rising 1,200 feet from its beginning. Anyone with heart or breathing problems should think twice about making this hike.

Camping

Please see camping descriptions for Eagle and Carbondale.

Chamber of Commerce, 1102 Grand Ave., Glenwood Springs 80601. Phone: 945-6589.

Emergency: 911.

U.S. Forest Service, 9th and Grand Ave. Phone: 945-6582.

Glenwood Springs

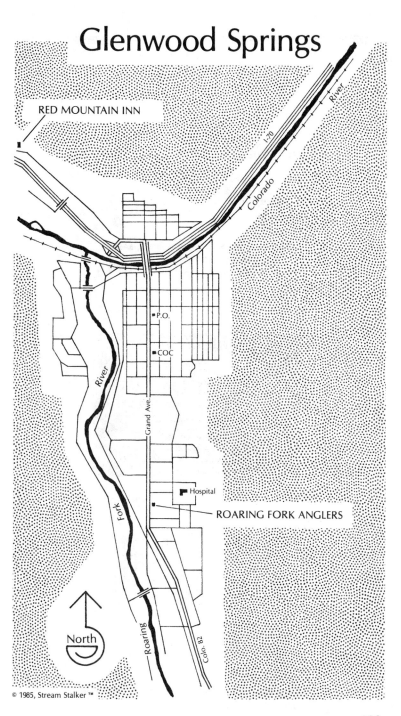

RED MOUNTAIN INN

L-70

Colorado

River

River

P.O.

COC

Grand Ave.

Hospital

ROARING FORK ANGLERS

Fork

Roaring

Colo. 82

North

© 1985, Stream Stalker ™

Glenwood Springs

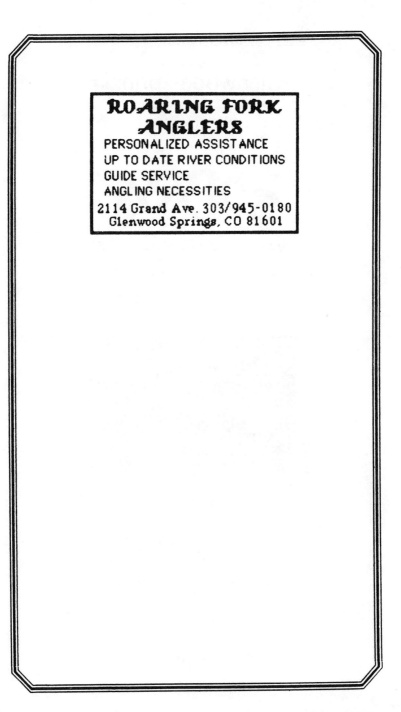

River Notes

SOUTH PLATTE RIVER

Map Reference 21

If any trout in Colorado were to be referred to as "smart," the fish of the South Platte River from Cheesman Reservoir down to Waterton Canyon would swim to the head of the class. The anglers of Denver and other Front Range communities who fish this river with regularity have taught these fish well, and the fish have the lip scars to prove it. They've been spooked and deceived and caught and released by some of the best anglers in Colorado. Their lessons have been remembered, and their inclination to reject an imitation of fur and feather is legend!

The South Platte gathers in South Park, where it meanders slugglishly across willow flats to the edge of the Front Range. Here it knifes through Eleven Mile Canyon, the Cheesman and Waterton canyons, before their granite walls reach out to meet the plains. As Denver's main water supply, the river has been the victim of many water projects, including the Cheesman Dam and Reservoir, the Antero Reservoir, and Eleven Mile Reservoir. In 1980, Spinney Mountain Dam was constructed just above Eleven Mile. Plans are now being considered to build the Two Forks Dam that will back the river water up the scenic North Fork seven miles to Foxton, and up the South Fork fifteen miles to past Deckers Resort. This would be the largest reservoir in the Colorado mountains, and to fill it will require water from the Western Slope.

193

Because of the fluctuating stream flows possible from day to day, it is a good idea to check with sports shops nearby to determine the volumes before you drive to the river. Average flows range between 100 and 200 cfs. It is running high when it is up to 400 to 700 cfs, and occasionally it will run 2,000 cfs. When water is high, fish the banks with nymphs just below the surface.

After turning off Old Highway 85 south of Denver onto County Road 67 heading west out of Sedalia, you will find the next sixteen miles to be winding and sometimes very steep. At mile 13.3 from Sedalia, the road splits at the settlement of Sprucewood. Road 67 continues to the left, and County Road 40 takes off to the right. The latter gravel road will take you down a rather interestingly steep hill, so keep your eyes open at mile 15, and take it easy if the road is wet. This road brings you out a bit lower on the river (4.5 miles lower) at the intersection called Nighthawk. When returning to Sedalia, you might wish to take Road 67 out, particularly if it is wet. Both Roads 67 and 40 intersect County Road 97 (Platte River Road), which parallels the river.

During average flows, the portion of the river from Nighthawk to Deckers is easy to wade and has but a nominal gradient. The road parallels the river, is alternately gravel and hardtop, but is all in good condition for passenger cars. Several picnic areas are available along the river.

From Deckers upstream on County Road 126 you climb toward the access to the "canyon water" below Cheesman Reservoir. At 1.7 miles from Deckers, you will see the boundary to the Wigwam Club. This is very private property of an exclusive fishing club, and trespassing is out of the question. Don't even ask! At 2.5 miles from Deckers, you will find a parking space at the head of the Gill Trail leading to the river above the Wigwam Club. This canyon area offers challenging fishing with small flies for educated fish. The river is filled with huge boulders, and pocket fishing is the rule, with deep holes and capricious currents keeping you alert at all times. If you continue past the Gill trailhead to mile 2.7, a narrow gravel road goes left up to the Cheesman Dam access at 5.6 miles. Plenty of parking space is available here, and a walk is necessary to the river below the dam.

Because of its close proximity to the major population densities of Colorado, the South Platte receives intense fishing pressure, particularly on the weekends. It is not unusual to wait in line at some favorite holding water for the opportunity to fish it. When the water is high, fishing is usually better in the canyon above the Wigwam Club up to the Cheesman Dam.

Insects

The majority of the South Platte aquatic insects are tiny. Artificials from size 18 down to 24 are standard, 26s and 28s are used, and 16s and larger are usually left at home, except for a few isolated patterns. When the water is low (60 to 100 cfs), long leaders (12 to 18 feet) are recommended, and tippet size down to 7X is standard. These fish see a lot of flies attached to numerous leaders attached to a lot of fishermen. Long, accurate, drag-free drifts are essential when tempting surface feeding fish. With nymphs in the deeper pools, one can approach somewhat closer, but careful wading is absolutely necessary. These fish are not tolerant of our mistakes and can humble the finest of anglers.

Wading is no problem in most of this river, as the bottom is not slick and much of it consists of fine gravel and small stones. We do, however, suggest using chest waders just for ease of moving about the river.

North Fork of the South Platte

Map Reference 21

Downstream from the Nighthawk intersection of Roads 40 and 97, to the intersection with the North Fork of the South Platte, there are 4.3 miles of public water. The North Fork is a typical Rocky Mountain freestone stream of twenty to thirty feet width, with tumbling riffles, tricky pockets, and occasional pools. This river fluctuates considerably, as does the South Fork, but can offer fair to good fishing when the water flow is normal.

Tackle

For the fly angler, a 4 or 5 weight outfit is all that is required. With the tiny dry flies and matching tippets used so often here, a softer, shock-absorbent rod is usually preferred. Leaders up to eighteen feet are suggested if you can throw them; if not, use as long as you can.

Flies and Lures

Dries—Griffith's Gnat, No. 18-22, R.S. 2, Nos. 20 and 22, Lt. Blue Quill No. 20, Grey Baetis No. 18. Tie your dries quite sparse for this water.

Nymphs—Rusty Scud No. 12, Pheasant Tail Nos. 18-22, Brassie Nos. 18 and 20, A.P. Nymph, Grey or Dark Olive, Nos. 16-20, Breadcrust Nos. 14-18, and Golden Stone Nymph, Nos. 14 and 16.

Lures—Dark colors in Rooster Tails, Panther Martin ⅛ to ¼ oz., and Mepps Spinners.

Camping

Because there is no write-up on a developed community along this river, we have included the camping information with the river description.

Several picnic grounds are situated along the river, but camping sites are not as numerous. Lone Rock Campground is located one mile west of Deckers and is the only campground on the river itself, so don't plan too seriously on being able to find a site when you want one. Better opportunity lies south on Highway 67 toward Woodland Park, twenty-three miles from Deckers. Lone Rock is small and receives very heavy use throughout the spring to fall seasons.

We urge extreme caution with fires in this area, as seasonal winds combined with the dry, warm climate raise the fire danger considerably. A fire lookout tower rests on the summit of Devil's Head Mountain at the north end of the Rampart Range here, and visitors are welcome. The tower is reached by hiking one and one-half miles along the Devil's Head National Recreational Trail.

Denver

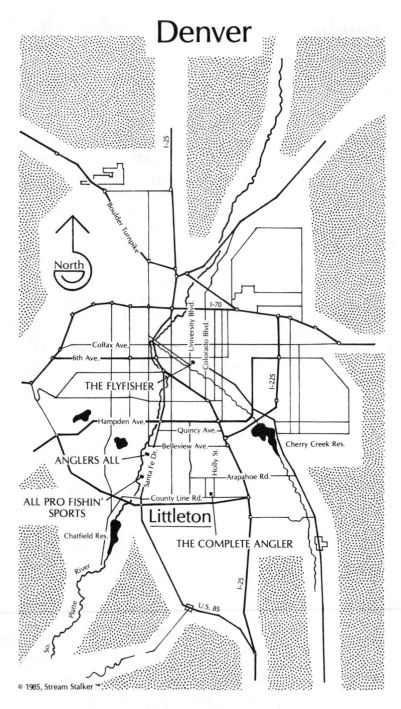

North

I-25

Boulder Turnpike

I-70

University Blvd.

Colorado Blvd.

I-225

Colfax Ave.

6th Ave.

THE FLYFISHER

Hampden Ave.

Quincy Ave.

Belleview Ave.

Cherry Creek Res.

ANGLERS ALL

Santa Fe Dr.

Holly St.

Arapahoe Rd.

ALL PRO FISHIN' SPORTS

County Line Rd.

Littleton

Chatfield Res.

THE COMPLETE ANGLER

River

U.S. 85

So. Platte

Denver

TAYLOR RIVER

Map Reference 8

The Taylor is a mover! It waits for nothing in its tumbling journey from the dam at Taylor Park Reservoir to its mating with the East, giving birth to the Gunnison River. The actual beginnings of the Taylor start at 11,800 feet in the Elk Mountains as a gathering of several streams flowing into the reservoir. The watercourse below the dam is approximately fifty feet wide, and the water is very cold due to the bottom release from the dam.

Water volume in the river ranges from 100 to 400 cfs. When at lower volumes of 100 to 200 cfs, the river is quite wadable, but it really gets tough at 200 to 400 cfs. The bottom is slippery anyway, but with an average gradient of 60 feet per mile, wading can be difficult even with the use of metal cleats. There's always the chance of stepping off into deep water.

The river is paralleled by State Highway 306 down through the granitic rocks, willows, and bushy alders. The resident fish include browns, rainbows, brooks, and the occasional cutthroat. River levels fluctuate during the spring, and on occasion the river can be quite fishable while other rivers are at their highest levels. By July, it has usually stabilized to a normal flow.

About 60 percent of the river in the twenty miles below the dam is open to public fishing. From Lottis Creek to the dam is private, as is the water below Spring Creek. This creek has fairly good fishing in its lower reaches from the campground upstream for three to four miles.

The angling technique used on the Taylor usually involves short line fishing in the pockets between boulders. This is not a riffle/pool type river, so nymph fishing is often more effective than dry fly. Insect life is abundant, with plenty of caddis, stoneflies, and mayflies.

Tackle

For flyfishing, five and six weight lines will do the job nicely. For spinning, four-pound lines are standard. Equipment and guide services are available in Gunnison, Almont, and Crested Butte.

Flies and Lures

Caddis imitations work well here—Elk Hair Caddis, Goddard Caddis, both in Nos. 14 and 16. It is important that the dries float well in this fast water, so high quality hackle and water-repellent materials are a must. Important nymphs include the Hare's Ear, Olive and Green Caddis larvae, peacock herl patterns, and brown stonefly nymphs in sizes 6 to 10.

Lures—Gold and silver Mepps, Black Vibrax, and Panther Martins in Salamander and Black.

Taylor Park Reservoir

This body of water lies thirty miles northwest of Gunnison at an elevation of 9,330 feet. Boats are available for rent, and motors are allowed on this reservoir of four miles by two miles. Fish here include browns, rainbows, brooks, kokanee salmon, and lake trout. Best times to fly and spin fish here are early and late, through June and then again in September and October. During the warm summer months, trolling deep is most effective.

River Notes

River Notes

Acknowledgments

Having been serious fishermen for many years, we feel that being an enthusiastic angler and getting involved with the many facets of the sport eventually enrich one's overall well-being and reinforce those subtle characteristics that make up one's personality. In addition to learning how to cast a line, wade a river, and read the water, we also delve into the many mysterious aspects of nature that fascinate our curiosity and challenge our thinking. We study to a greater or lesser extent those straightforward physiological characteristics of fish and their prey, and try to understand the subtle instinctive trigger mechanisms that motivate trout to react the way they do to the environment that surrounds them.

We tie flies, make lures, build rods, improve habitat, join conservation organizations, write articles, read articles, buy books, contemplate theories, improve skills, try new ideas, teach techniques, tell stories, and for many of us, get thoroughly involved in the pursuit of trying to deceive a fish. To the nonfisherman, we probably appear totally irresponsible and completely irrational! If that be so, so be it. But we members of this fraternity know in our souls that life can be a lot better when we are out fishing than when we're not.

Our sport takes on even greater personal meaning when we can share our knowledge, ideas, experiences, and enthusiasm with others who understand our feelings. The camaraderie between fishermen truly enhances the satisfaction we gain from our own experience. Sharing knowledge and zeal with others amplifies the rewards we reap from our angling efforts. While traveling throughout Colorado compiling data for this guide, we had the good fortune to talk to many old friends and meet many new ones. The anglers we acknowledge here made this guide a more viable work than it might otherwise have been. They shared insights they had gained after many years of fishing Colorado's waters, and we all benefit from their experience. They truly welcomed the opportunity to contribute their expertise to others who might not know as much about their home waters as they do. Some of these men are involved in the fishing industry as a means of livelihood; others enjoy fishing strictly as an avocation. But one thing is common in the attitude they all display toward the sport—they know a conservation ethic must be practiced by anglers if fishing for wild trout is to be enjoyed in the future. These anglers enjoy living fish—not dead ones. They enjoy water that is cold, clear, and pure, not the tainted fluid so often left by commercial interests in their careless pursuit of profit. These gentlemen take their sport seriously, yet make it a great deal of fun. They study the sport to enable them to catch many fish under all conditions, yet they wish to do the fish no harm. They realize that preservation of trout and trout habitat will preserve the pleasure they receive from their time spent casting a fly. Killing trout and destroying habitat simply deteriorate that pleasure.

The anglers listed below are sportsmen in the true sense of the word, and we're proud to know them. Thank you, gentlemen!

Ray Armstrong	Steve Hix	Jerry Swan
Rick Baur	Hank Hotze	Dean Teegarden
Russ Bybee	Dave Kenvin	Ed Valdez
Del Canty	Jack Kenyon	
Pat Carlow	Roark Kiklevich	
Gary Cyr	Gary Lore	
Don Gore	Harry Love	
Bill Grems	Dave Luke	
Mike Gula	Larry Mathena	
Carey Griffin	Bill Porterfield	
Bill Haberlein	Dean Prentiss	
Steve Herter	Scott Roederer	
Ethan Hicks	Bill Shappell	
Glen Hinshaw	Jackson Streit	

Colorado Information Sources

COLORADO DIVISION OF WILDLIFE
6060 Broadway, Denver 80216 297-1192

U.S. FOREST SERVICE
P.O. Box 25127, Lakewood 80225 234-4185

COLORADO DIVISION OF PARKS AND
OUTDOOR RECREATION
1313 Sherman St., Denver 80203 839-3437

U.S. BUREAU OF LAND MANAGEMENT
1037 20th St., Denver 80202 837-4481

U.S. GEOLOGICAL SURVEY
P.O. Box 25286, Denver 80225 234-3832

COLORADO CAMPGROUND ASSOCIATION
5101 Pennsylvania Ave., Boulder 80303 499-9343

COLORADO HIGHWAY DEPARTMENT
4201 E. Arkansas Ave., Denver 80222 757-9011

THE NATIONAL PARK SERVICE
655 Parfet St., P.O. Box 25287, Lakewood 80215 234-3095

COLORADO DIVISION OF COMMERCE AND DEVELOPMENT
Travel Marketing Section
5500 S. Syracuse, Englewood 80111 779-1067

CUMBRES & TOLTEC SCENIC RAILROAD (reservations
   required)
P.O. Box 789
Chama, New Mexico 87520 (505) 756-2151
(operated by the states of Colorado & New Mexico)

DURANGO-SILVERTON NARROW GAUGE
RAILROAD COMPANY
479 Main Ave., Durango 81301 247-2733
(operated by the state of Colorado)

COLORADO STATE MUSEUM AND HISTORICAL SOCIETY
1300 Broadway, Denver 80203 866-4682

COLORADO GOLF ASSOCIATION
1777 So. Bellaire, Denver 80222 759-9502

COLORADO TENNIS ASSOCIATION
1201 So. Parker Road, Denver 80231 695-4116

COLORADO HEART ASSOCIATION
4521 East Virginia Ave., Denver 80222 399-2131

	WALDEN	VAIL	SALIDA	LEADVILLE	HOT SULPHUR SPGS	GUNNISON	GLENWOOD SPCS	FORT COLLINS	ESTES PARK	DENVER	CREEDE	CANON CITY	BUENA VISTA	BRECKENRIDGE	ASPEN	ANTONITO	ALAMOSA
ALAMOSA	267	172	83	134	223	122	204	274	280	212	68	139	100	154	163	28	
ANTONITO	295	190	111	162	251	150	232	302	308	240	96	165	128	182	191		
ASPEN	194	102	88	59	150	146	41	223	204	162	201	145	63	100			
BRECKENRIDGE	113	36	80	41	69	138	97	141	123	81	192	96	245				
BUENA VISTA	170	62	26	34	126	83	104	179	185	117	138	82					
CANON CITY	210	133	57	117	166	121	187	177	183	115	176						
CREEDE	306	210	121	172	262	107	242	313	318	251							
DENVER	143	98	138	103	97	196	159	65	71								
ESTES PARK	117	140	207	145	265	196	196	42									
FORT COLLINS	99	159	200	164	258	220	220										
GLENWOOD SPRINGS	185	61	130	89	125	162											
GUNNISON	251	156	66	118	207												
HOT SULPHUR SPRINGS	61	104	149	91													
LEADVILLE	135	38	60														
SALIDA	193	98															
VAIL	140																
WALDEN																	

Bibliography

Chronic, Halka, *Roadside Geology*, Mountain Press, 1980.

Kelley, Tim, *Tim Kelley's Fishing Guide*, Hart Publications, Inc., 1983.

Murray, Robert B., and Lee, Russell D., *Colorado Ghost Town Guide*, Colorado Recreation Guides, 1982.

Wheat, Doug, *The Floater's Guide to Colorado*, Falcon Press, 1983.

Brochures, Pamphlets, and Maps Provided By:
Chambers of Commerce throughout Colorado
Colorado Division of Commerce and Development
Colorado Division of Parks and Outdoor Recreation
Colorado Division of Wildlife
United States Forest Service

Index

215

ORDER FORM

Gentlemen:

Please send me ___ copy (ies) of **The Colorado Angling Guide**. I have enclosed a check or money order payable to Stream Stalker in the amount of **$14.95** for each copy plus $1.00 shipping and handling fee. (Colorado residents add $.54 [3½%] tax per copy.)

(Please type or print)

Name_____

Mailing Address _____

City_____

State and Zip Code _____

Amount Enclosed_____

STREAM STALKER, BOX 1010, Aspen, Colorado 81612

TO OUR READERS

A book is always a welcome gift! Particularly if the book will help the recipient enjoy one of his favorite pastimes. If you have a fisherman friend, a gift of **The Colorado Angling Guide** would be a welcome addition to his angling/travel library.

Show him you wish him "good luck" before he starts his next Colorado fishing trip. Help him maximize his angling hours by learning in advance what he and/or his family needs to know about Colorado's finest trout streams and the towns that serve them.

One other consideration—if he has his own copy, he won't be borrowing yours!!

TO OUR READERS

A book is always a welcome gift! Particularly if the book will help the recipient enjoy one of his favorite pastimes. If you have a fisherman friend, a gift of **The Colorado Angling Guide** would be a welcome addition to his angling/travel library.

Show him you wish him "good luck" before he starts his next Colorado fishing trip. Help him maximize his angling hours by learning in advance what he and/or his family needs to know about Colorado's finest trout streams and the towns that serve them.

One other consideration—if he has his own copy, he won't be borrowing yours!

ORDER FORM

Gentlemen:

Please send me ___ copy (ies) of **The Colorado Angling Guide**. I have enclosed a check or money order payable to Stream Stalker in the amount of **$14.95** for each copy plus $1.00 shipping and handling fee. (Colorado residents add $.54 [3½%] tax per copy.)

(Please type or print)

Name_____

Mailing Address _____

City_____

State and Zip Code _____

Amount Enclosed _____

STREAM STALKER, BOX 1010, Aspen, Colorado 81612

Part II:

River Maps

MAPS

The river and town maps are schematic. In the interest of brevity, only those items of information important to the fisherman are shown. Roads and highways are shown without all curves and bends, but bridge crossings, intersections, and other details are depicted as accurately as scale permits.

Mileage markers on roads and highways next to rivers identify significant points of interest to the fisherman and are explained on the maps.

Where available, the locations of essential services on the town maps, including locations of advertisers, are indicated.

VICINITY MAP

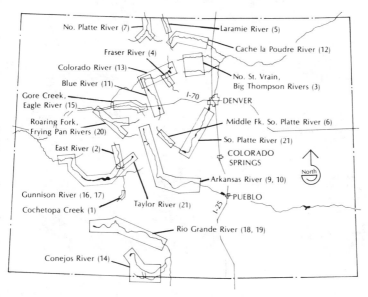

No. Platte River (7)
Laramie River (5)
Cache la Poudre River (12)
Fraser River (4)
Colorado River (13)
No. St. Vrain,
Big Thompson Rivers (3)
Blue River (11)
Gore Creek,
Eagle River (15)
I-70
DENVER
Roaring Fork,
Frying Pan Rivers (20)
Middle Fk. So. Platte River (6)
East River (2)
So. Platte River (21)
COLORADO
SPRINGS
North
Gunnison River (16, 17)
Arkansas River (9, 10)
Cochetopa Creek (1)
Taylor River (21)
I-25
PUEBLO
Rio Grande River (18, 19)
Conejos River (14)

COLORADO

LEGEND

Campgrounds, Picnic Grounds	■
Improved roads	=
Unimproved roads, 4WD	====
Hiking trails	------
Access points	O
Small settlements, limited services	·:⁙·
Towns described in text	⊐
Gold Medal Water	☐
Wild Trout Water	⊏⊐

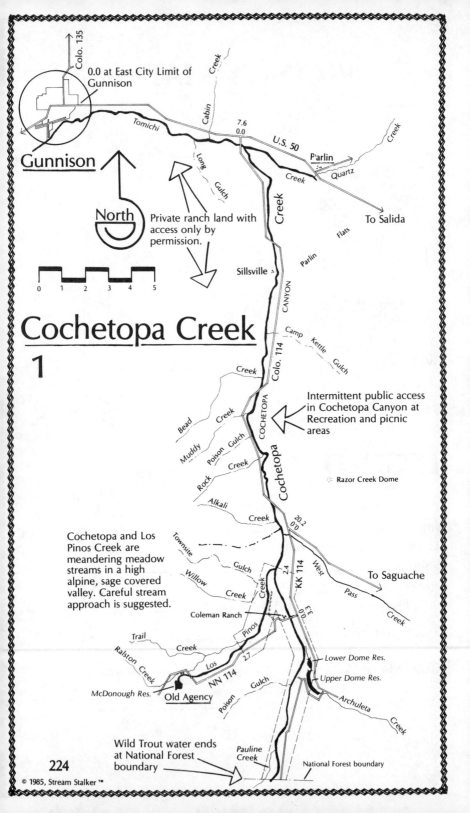

Colo. 135

0.0 at East City Limit of Gunnison

Creek

Cabin

7.6
0.0

U.S. 50

P'arlin

Creek

Quartz

Gunnison

Tomichi

Long

Gulch

Creek

Creek

To Salida

North

Private ranch land with access only by permission.

Flats

Parlin

Sillsville

CANYON

Colo. 114

Camp

Kettle

Gulch

Cochetopa Creek
1

0 1 2 3 4 5

Creek

COCHETOPA

Intermittent public access in Cochetopa Canyon at Recreation and picnic areas

Bead

Creek

Cochetopa

Muddy

Poison Gulch

Razor Creek Dome

Rock

Creek

Alkali

Creek

20.2
0.0

Cochetopa and Los Pinos Creek are meandering meadow streams in a high alpine, sage covered valley. Careful stream approach is suggested.

Townsite

Gulch

Creek

KK 114

West

Pass

To Saguache

Willow

Creek

2.4

0.0
3.3

Coleman Ranch

Creek

Trail

Creek

Pinos

Lower Dome Res.

Ralston Creek

Los

2.7

Upper Dome Res.

McDonough Res.

NN 114

Poison

Gulch

Archuleta

Creek

Old Agency

Wild Trout water ends at National Forest boundary

Pauline

Creek

National Forest boundary

224

© 1985, Stream Stalker ™

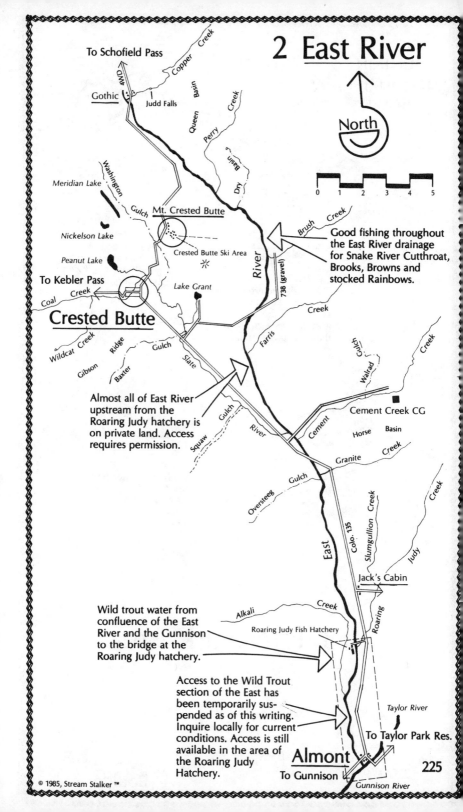

2 East River

North

0 1 2 3 4 5

To Schofield Pass

Copper Creek

Gothic

Judd Falls

Queen Basin Creek

Perry Creek

Dry Basin

Brush Creek

Good fishing throughout the East River drainage for Snake River Cutthroat, Brooks, Browns and stocked Rainbows.

Meridian Lake

Washington Gulch

Mt. Crested Butte

Crested Butte Ski Area

Nickelson Lake

Peanut Lake

To Kebler Pass

Coal Creek

Lake Grant

River

738 (gravel)

Creek

Crested Butte

Wildcat Creek

Gibson Ridge

Baxter

Gulch

Slate

Farris

Gulch

Walrad

Creek

Cement Creek CG

Horse Basin

Creek

Almost all of East River upstream from the Roaring Judy hatchery is on private land. Access requires permission.

Squaw Gulch

River

Cement

Granite Creek

Oversteeg Gulch

Slumgullion Creek

Creek

Judy

Creek

East

Colo. 135

Jack's Cabin

Wild trout water from confluence of the East River and the Gunnison to the bridge at the Roaring Judy hatchery.

Alkali Creek

Roaring Judy Fish Hatchery

Roaring

Access to the Wild Trout section of the East has been temporarily suspended as of this writing. Inquire locally for current conditions. Access is still available in the area of the Roaring Judy Hatchery.

Taylor River

To Taylor Park Res.

Almont

To Gunnison

Gunnison River

225

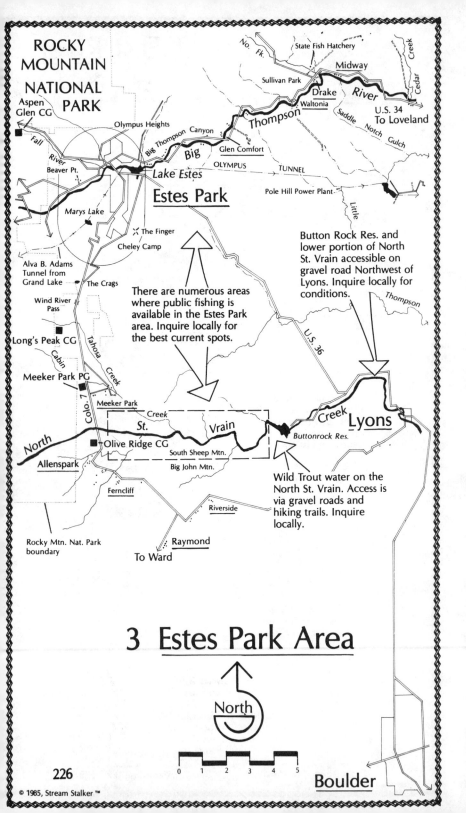

ROCKY MOUNTAIN NATIONAL PARK

Aspen Glen CG

Fall River

Beaver Pt.

Olympus Heights

Marys Lake

The Finger
Cheley Camp

Alva B. Adams Tunnel from Grand Lake

The Crags

Wind River Pass

Long's Peak CG

Cabin

Meeker Park PG

Meeker Park

Colo. 7

Tahosa Creek

Olive Ridge CG

Allenspark

North

Ferncliff

Rocky Mtn. Nat. Park boundary

Big Thompson Canyon

Big

Glen Comfort

OLYMPUS

Lake Estes

Estes Park

No. Fk.

State Fish Hatchery

Midway

Sullivan Park

Drake

Waltonia

Thompson River

Saddle Notch Gulch

Cedar Creek

U.S. 34 To Loveland

TUNNEL

Pole Hill Power Plant

Little

Button Rock Res. and lower portion of North St. Vrain accessible on gravel road Northwest of Lyons. Inquire locally for conditions.

Thompson

U.S. 36

There are numerous areas where public fishing is available in the Estes Park area. Inquire locally for the best current spots.

St. Vrain

Creek

Creek

Lyons

Buttonrock Res.

South Sheep Mtn.

Big John Mtn.

Riverside

Raymond

To Ward

Wild Trout water on the North St. Vrain. Access is via gravel roads and hiking trails. Inquire locally.

3 Estes Park Area

North

0 1 2 3 4 5

Boulder

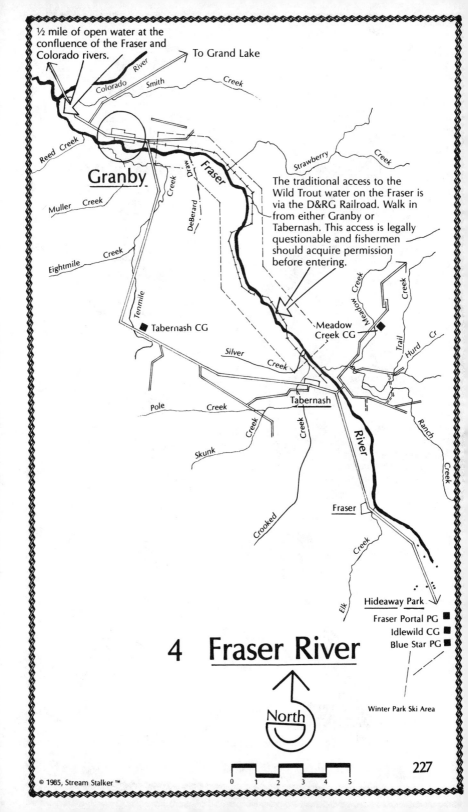

½ mile of open water at the confluence of the Fraser and Colorado rivers.

To Grand Lake

Colorado River

Smith Creek

Reed Creek

Granby

Muller Creek

Eightmile Creek

Draw Creek

DeBerard Creek

Fraser

Strawberry Creek

The traditional access to the Wild Trout water on the Fraser is via the D&RG Railroad. Walk in from either Granby or Tabernash. This access is legally questionable and fishermen should acquire permission before entering.

Meadow Creek

Trail Creek

Hurd Cr

Tenmile

■ Tabernash CG

Meadow Creek CG ◆

Silver Creek

Pole Creek

Creek

Creek

River

Tabernash

Ranch Creek

Skunk Creek

Crooked Creek

Fraser

Elk Creek

Hideaway Park

Fraser Portal PG ■
Idlewild CG ■
Blue Star PG ■

Winter Park Ski Area

4 **Fraser River**

North

0 1 2 3 4 5

227

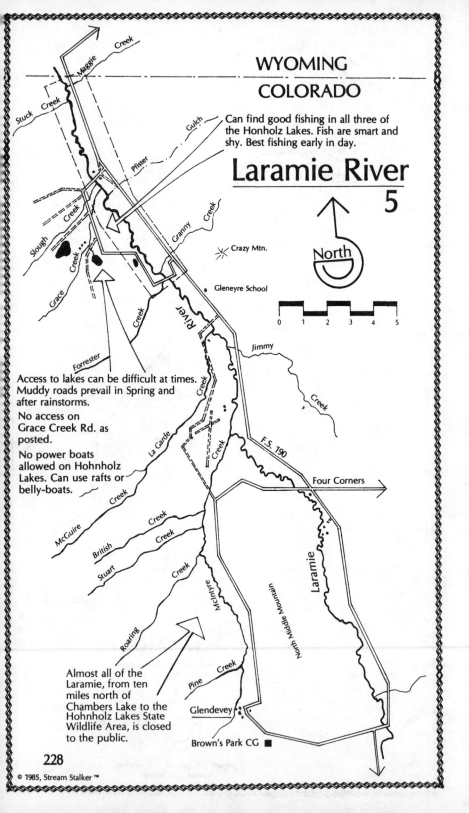

WYOMING

COLORADO

Can find good fishing in all three of the Honholz Lakes. Fish are smart and shy. Best fishing early in day.

Laramie River
5

North

0 1 2 3 4 5

Crazy Mtn.

Gleneyre School

Maggie Creek

Stuck Creek

Gulch

Pfister

Creek

Granny Creek

Slough Creek

Grace Creek

Forrester Creek

River

Jimmy Creek

Access to lakes can be difficult at times. Muddy roads prevail in Spring and after rainstorms.

No access on Grace Creek Rd. as posted.

No power boats allowed on Hohnholz Lakes. Can use rafts or belly-boats.

La Carde Creek

Creek

F.S. 190

Four Corners

McGuire Creek

British Creek

Stuart Creek

Laramie

North Middle Mountain

McIntyre Creek

Roaring Creek

Pine Creek

Almost all of the Laramie, from ten miles north of Chambers Lake to the Hohnholz Lakes State Wildlife Area, is closed to the public.

Glendevey

Brown's Park CG ■

228

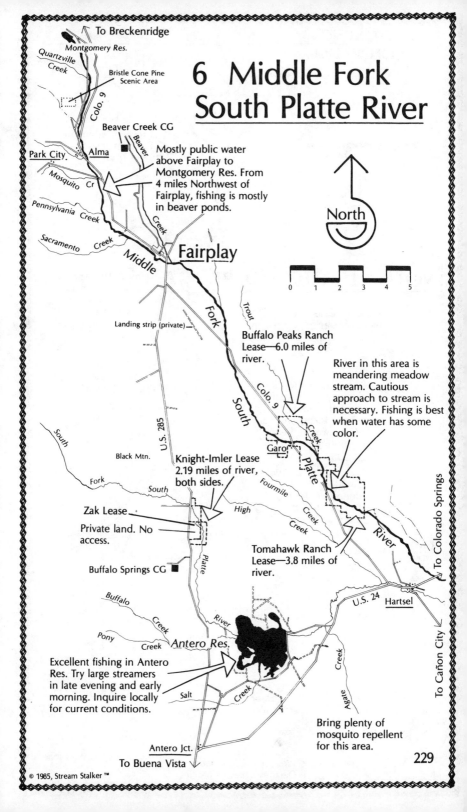

To Breckenridge

Montgomery Res.

Quartzville Creek

Bristle Cone Pine
Scenic Area

Beaver Creek CG

6 Middle Fork
South Platte River

Park City. Alma

Mosquito Cr

Beaver Creek

Pennsylvania Creek

Sacramento Creek

Middle

Mostly public water
above Fairplay to
Montgomery Res. From
4 miles Northwest of
Fairplay, fishing is mostly
in beaver ponds.

North

0 1 2 3 4 5

Fairplay

Fork

Trout

Landing strip (private)

Buffalo Peaks Ranch
Lease—6.0 miles of
river.

River in this area is
meandering meadow
stream. Cautious
approach to stream is
necessary. Fishing is best
when water has some
color.

South

Colo. 9

Creek

Platte

Garo

U.S. 285

Black Mtn.

South

Fork

South

High

Knight-Imler Lease
2.19 miles of river,
both sides.

Fourmile

Creek

River

Zak Lease

Private land. No
access.

Buffalo Springs CG

Platte

Creek

Tomahawk Ranch
Lease—3.8 miles of
river.

To Colorado Springs

Buffalo

Creek

Pony

Creek

River

Antero Res.

U.S. 24 Hartsel

Excellent fishing in Antero
Res. Try large streamers
in late evening and early
morning. Inquire locally
for current conditions.

Salt

Creek

Creek

Agate

To Cañon City

Bring plenty of
mosquito repellent
for this area.

Antero Jct.

To Buena Vista

229

© 1985, Stream Stalker ™

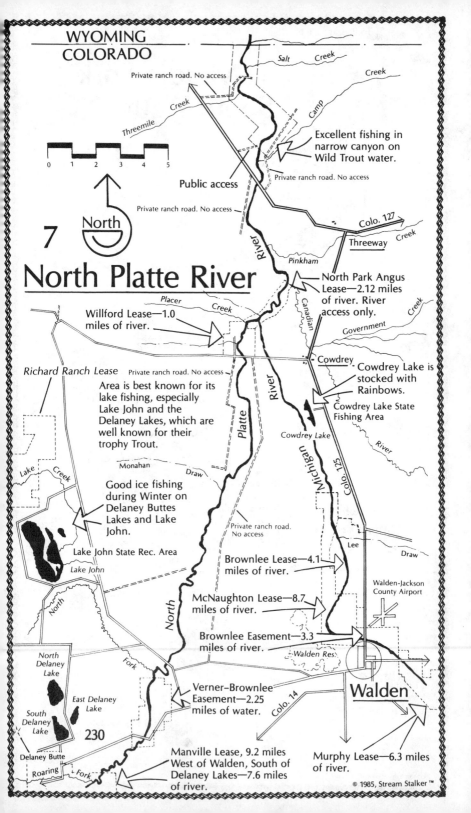

WYOMING
COLORADO

Private ranch road. No access

Salt Creek

Creek

Creek

Camp

Threemile

Excellent fishing in
narrow canyon on
Wild Trout water.

Public access

Private ranch road. No access

Private ranch road. No access

Colo. 127

Threeway Creek

River

Pinkham

7

North

North Platte River

0 1 2 3 4 5

Placer Creek

Willford Lease—1.0
miles of river.

North Park Angus
Lease—2.12 miles
of river. River
access only.

Richard Ranch Lease   Private ranch road. No access

Canadian

Government Creek

Cowdrey

Cowdrey Lake is
stocked with
Rainbows.

Area is best known for its
lake fishing, especially
Lake John and the
Delaney Lakes, which are
well known for their
trophy Trout.

Platte River

Michigan

Cowdrey Lake

Cowdrey Lake State
Fishing Area

Lake Creek

Monahan Draw

River

Good ice fishing
during Winter on
Delaney Buttes
Lakes and Lake
John.

Private ranch road.
No access

Lake John State Rec. Area

Lake John

Colo. 125

Lee Draw

Brownlee Lease—4.1
miles of river.

North

McNaughton Lease—8.7
miles of river.

Walden-Jackson
County Airport

Brownlee Easement—3.3
miles of river.

Walden Res.

North
Delaney
Lake

Fork

Verner-Brownlee
Easement—2.25
miles of water.

Walden

East Delaney
Lake

South
Delaney
Lake

Colo. 14

230

Delaney Butte

Roaring Fork

Manville Lease, 9.2 miles
West of Walden, South of
Delaney Lakes—7.6 miles
of river.

Murphy Lease—6.3 miles
of river.

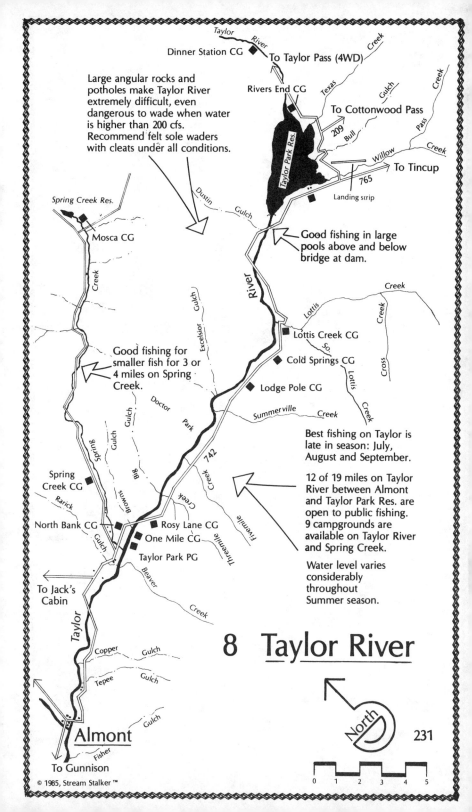

Taylor River

To Taylor Pass (4WD)

Dinner Station CG

Rivers End CG

To Cottonwood Pass

Large angular rocks and potholes make Taylor River extremely difficult, even dangerous to wade when water is higher than 200 cfs. Recommend felt sole waders with cleats under all conditions.

Texas Gulch Creek

209

Bull

Taylor Park Res.

Willow Creek

To Tincup

765

Landing strip

Spring Creek Res.

Dustin Gulch

Mosca CG

Good fishing in large pools above and below bridge at dam.

Creek

River

Lottis Creek

Creek

Creek

Lottis Creek CG

So. Cross Creek

Lottis Creek

Cold Springs CG

Good fishing for smaller fish for 3 or 4 miles on Spring Creek.

Excelsior Gulch

Doctor Gulch

Gulch

Lodge Pole CG

Summerville Creek

Park

742

Best fishing on Taylor is late in season: July, August and September.

Spring Gulch

Big Gulch

Browns

Spring Creek CG

Creek

12 of 19 miles on Taylor River between Almont and Taylor Park Res. are open to public fishing. 9 campgrounds are available on Taylor River and Spring Creek.

Rarick

North Bank CG

Rosy Lane CG

One Mile CG

Taylor Park PG

Gulch

Threemile Creek

Fivemile Creek

Water level varies considerably throughout Summer season.

To Jack's Cabin

Beaver Creek

Taylor

Copper Gulch

8 Taylor River

Tepee Gulch

Gulch

Almont

North

231

To Gunnison

Fisher

© 1985, Stream Stalker ™

0 1 2 3 4 5